NAME ____________________ TAKE-HOME 1 SIDE 1

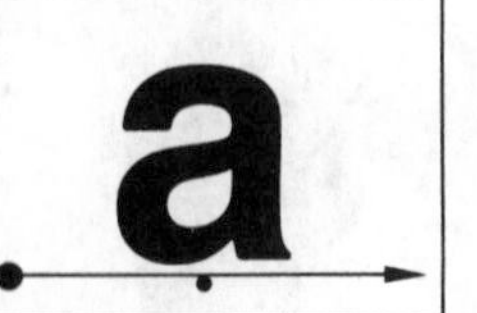

a a a a a a a

a a a a a a a

TAKE-HOME 1 SIDE 2

Printed in the United States of America

NAME ____________________ TAKE-HOME 2 SIDE 1

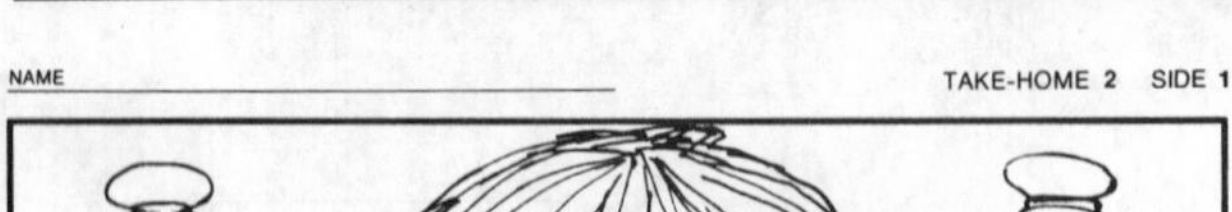

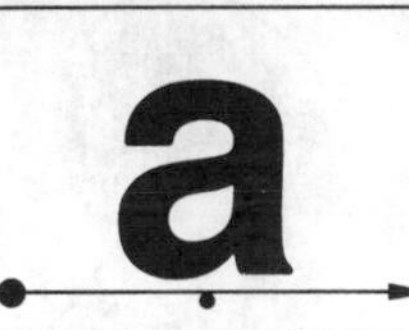

a a a a a a a

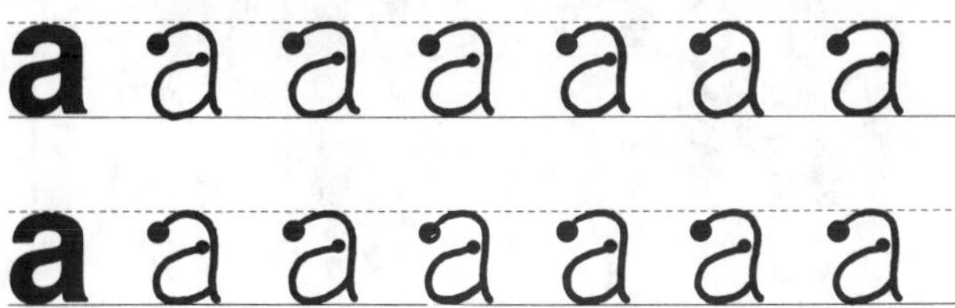

TAKE-HOME 2 SIDE 2

Printed in the United States of America

NAME ________________ TAKE-HOME 3 SIDE 1

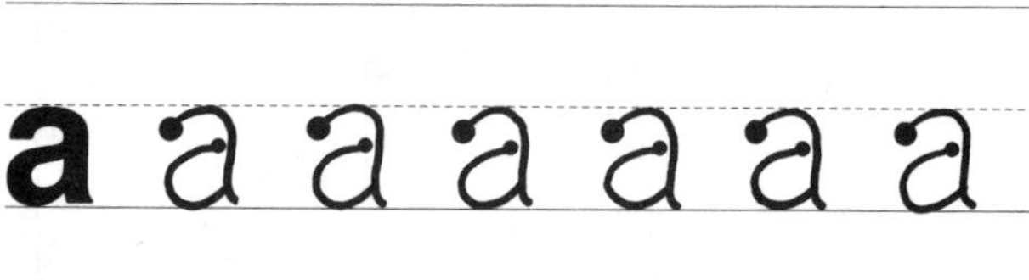

TAKE-HOME 3 SIDE 2

Printed in the United States of America

2

NAME ________________ TAKE-HOME 4 SIDE 1

a a a a a a a

a a a a a a a

TAKE-HOME 4 SIDE 2

Printed in the United States of America.

NAME

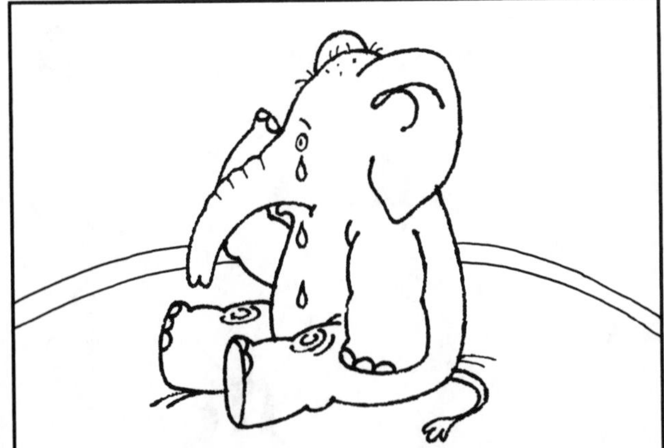

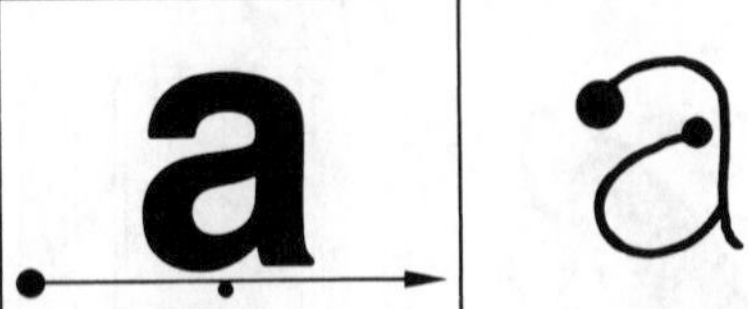

a a a a a a a

a a a a a a a

Printed in the United States of America

NAME

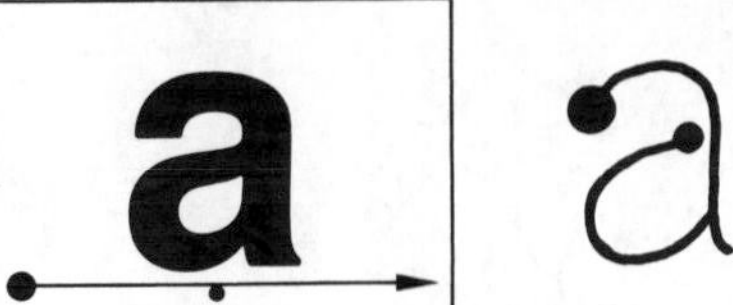

a a a a a a a

a a a a a a a

Printed in the United States of America

NAME ______________________________ TAKE-HOME **7** SIDE **1**

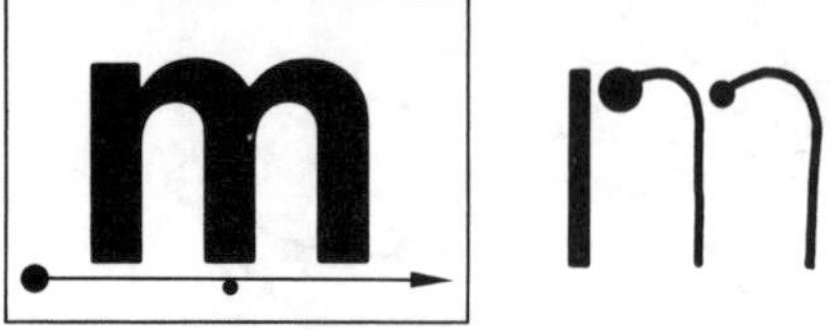

m

m

TAKE-HOME **7** SIDE **2**

Printed in the United States of America

NAME ______________________________ TAKE-HOME **8** SIDE **1**

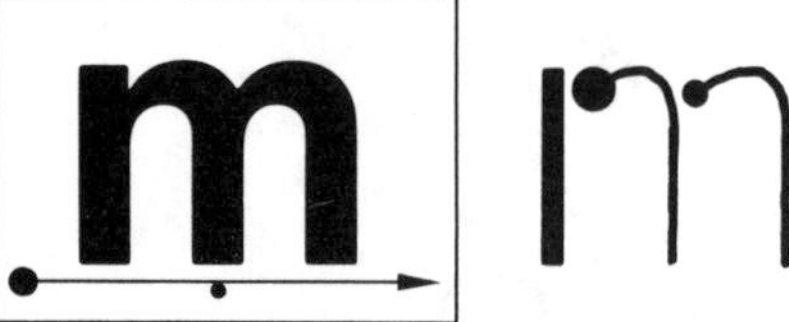

m

m

TAKE-HOME **8** SIDE **2**

Printed in the United States of America

NAME

TAKE-HOME 9 SIDE 1

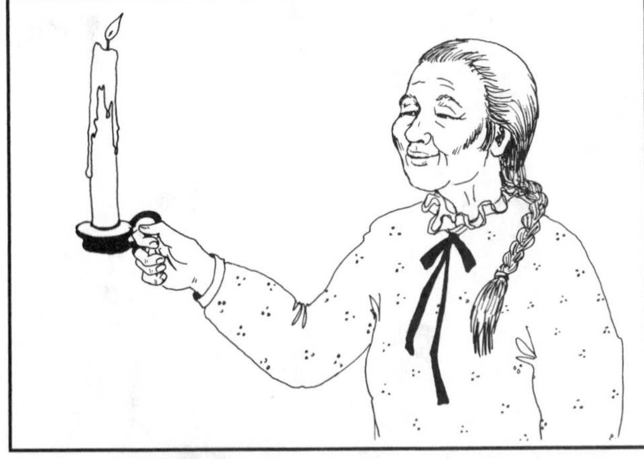

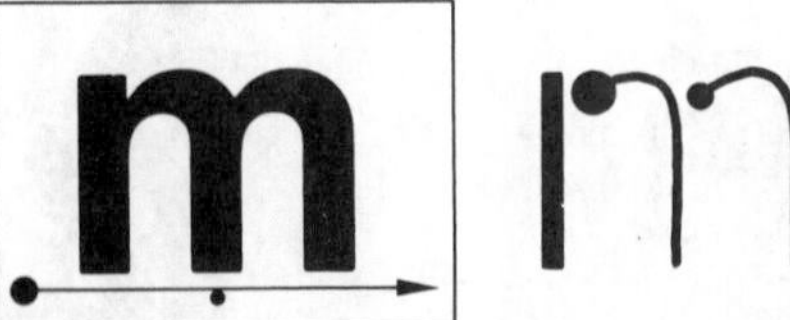

m m m m m m m

m m m m m m m

TAKE-HOME 9 SIDE 2

Printed in the United States of America

NAME

TAKE-HOME 10 SIDE 1

a a a a a a a

a a a a a a a

TAKE-HOME 10 SIDE 2

Printed in the United States of America

NAME ______________________ TAKE-HOME 11 SIDE 1

m m m m m m

m m m m m m

TAKE-HOME 11 SIDE 2

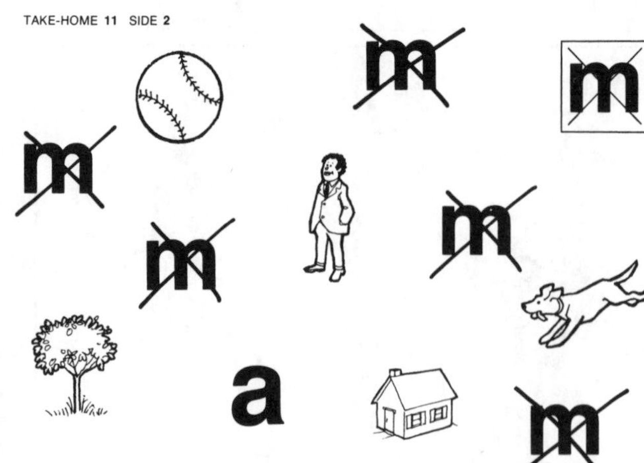

Printed in the United States of America.

NAME ______________________ TAKE-HOME 12 SIDE 1

m m m m m m

m m m m m m

TAKE-HOME 12 SIDE 2

Printed in the United States of America.

NAME ______________________

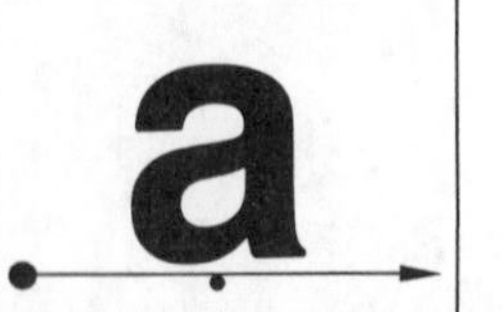

a a a a a a a

a a a a a a a

m a a a a a a

Printed in the United States of America

NAME ______________________

m

a a

a a a a a a a

a a a a a a a

a m a a a a a

Printed in the United States of America

NAME ________

TAKE-HOME 15 SIDE 1

a

m

m m m m m m

m m m m m m

TAKE-HOME 15 SIDE 2

Printed in the United States of America

NAME ________

TAKE-HOME 16 SIDE 1

m

a

a a a a a a a

a a a a a a a

TAKE-HOME 16 SIDE 2

Printed in the United States of America

NAME ____________________ TAKE-HOME **17** SIDE **1**

a

s

s

s s s s s s s

s s s s s s s

TAKE-HOME **17** SIDE **2**

Printed in the United States of America.

NAME ____________________ TAKE-HOME **18** SIDE **1**

m

s

s

s s s s s s s

s s s s s s s

TAKE-HOME **18** SIDE **2**

Printed in the United States of America.

NAME

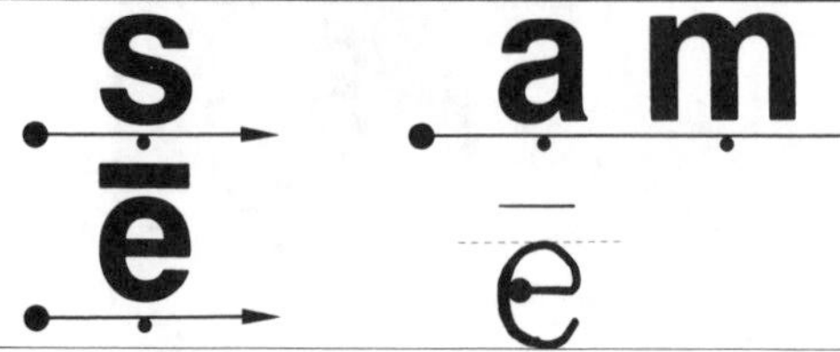

s am

ē ē

ē e e e e e e

ē e e e e e e

Printed in the United States of America

NAME

ē ma

s s

s s s s s s s

s s s s s s s

Printed in the United States of America

NAME ______________________

TAKE-HOME 21 SIDE 1

m ē

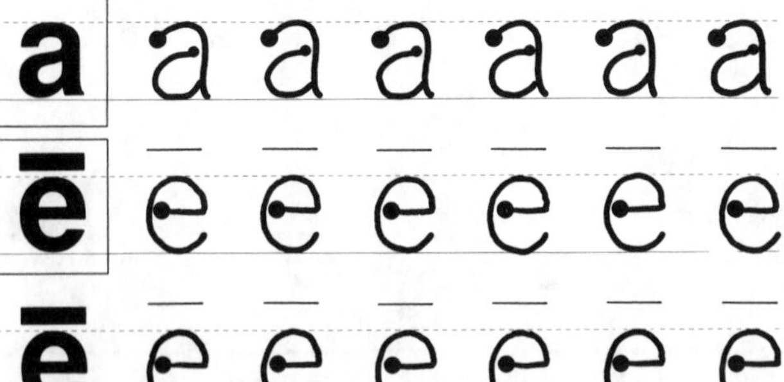

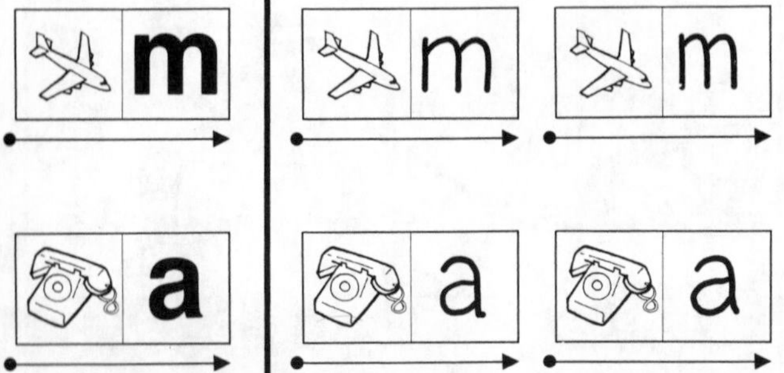

TAKE-HOME 21 SIDE 2

Printed in the United States of America

NAME ______________________

TAKE-HOME 22 SIDE 1

s a

ē e e e e e e

s s s s s s s

s s s s s s s

TAKE-HOME 22 SIDE 2

Printed in the United States of America

NAME ______________________ TAKE-HOME **23** SIDE 1

ē m

ē e e e e e e

m m m m m m

m m m m m m

 ē

 ē

 ē

 a

 a

 a

TAKE-HOME **23** SIDE 2

m a s m m m m m ē m m s m ē a m

Printed in the United States of America

12

NAME ______________________ TAKE-HOME **24** SIDE 1

s ē

a a a a a a a

r r r r r r r

r r r r r r r

 m

 m

 m

 s

 s

 s

TAKE-HOME **24** SIDE 2

r r r r s m r a m ē r r r r m

Printed in the United States of America

NAME 

TAKE-HOME **25** SIDE **1**

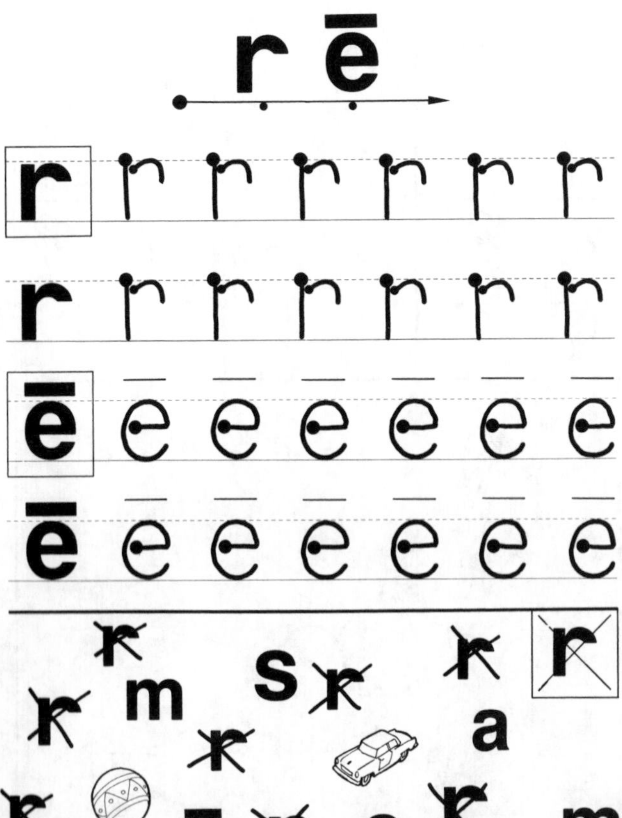

TAKE-HOME **25** SIDE **2**

Printed in the United States of America.

NAME

TAKE-HOME **26** SIDE **1**

ē r

m m m m m m m

m m m m m m m

s s s s s s s

s s s s s s s

m ē a a s a a m a r a a ē a

TAKE-HOME **26** SIDE **2**

Printed in the United States of America

NAME

TAKE-HOME 27 SIDE 1

r a

ē e e e e e e

ē e e e e e e

a a a a a a a

a a a a a a a

m s m m m ē s m a r r m m m

TAKE-HOME 27 SIDE 2

m 

r

Printed in the United States of America

14

NAME

TAKE-HOME 28 SIDE 1

m ē

r r r r r r r

r r r r r r r

d d d d d d d

d d d d d d d

d s m d d d ē d d a a d r d

TAKE-HOME 28 SIDE 2

s S S

ē

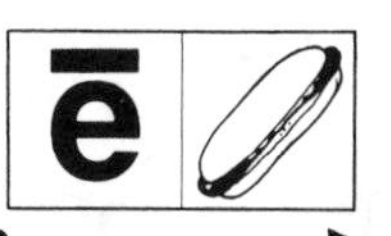

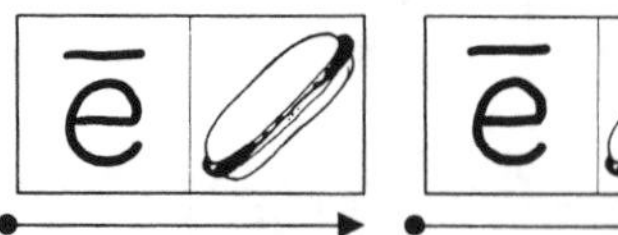

Printed in the United States of America

NAME

TAKE-HOME 29 SIDE 1

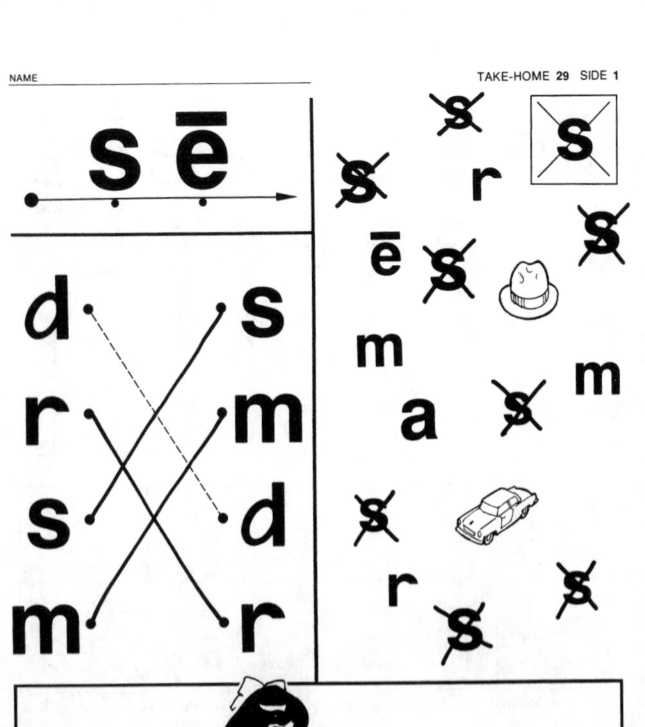

TAKE-HOME 29 SIDE 2

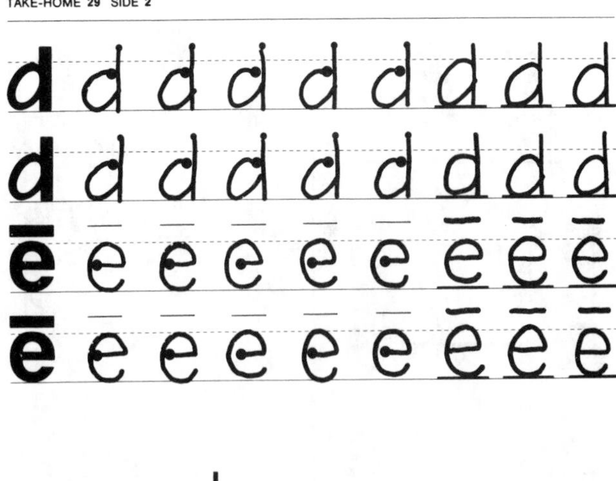

Printed in the United States of America

NAME

TAKE-HOME 30 SIDE 1

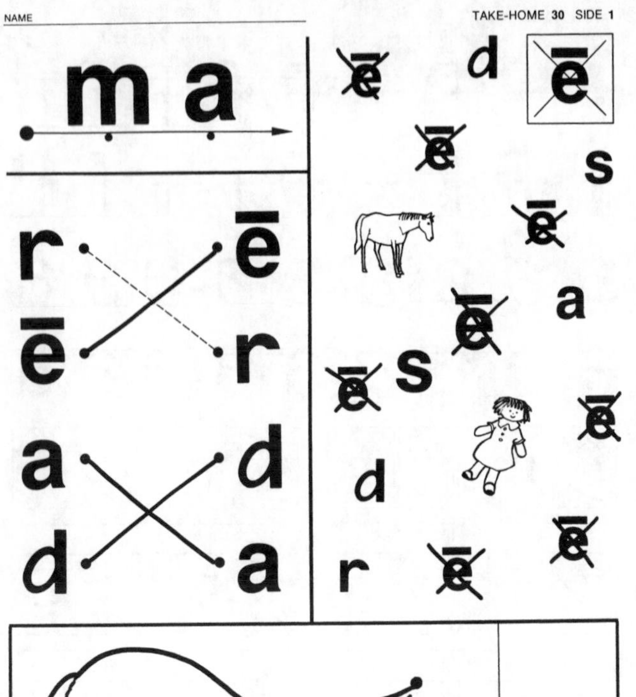

TAKE-HOME 30 SIDE 2

m m m m m m m

m m m m m m m

s s s s s s s s

s s s s s s s s

s s s s

a a a a

m m m m

r r r r

Printed in the United States of America

NAME ____________________

TAKE-HOME **31** SIDE **1**

r a

s	m
a	a
d	s
m	*d*

ē r s s d s ē s

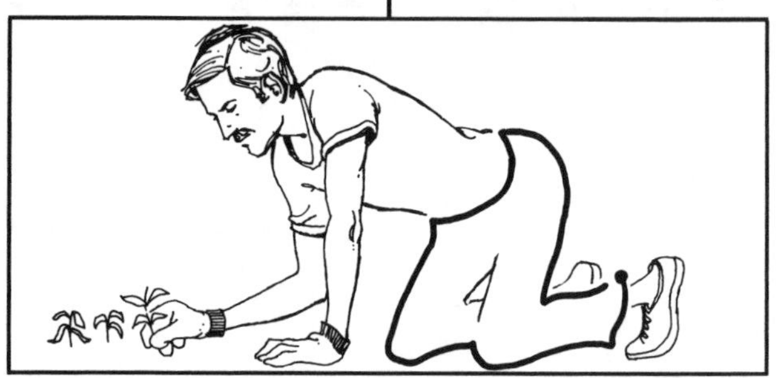

TAKE-HOME **31** SIDE 2

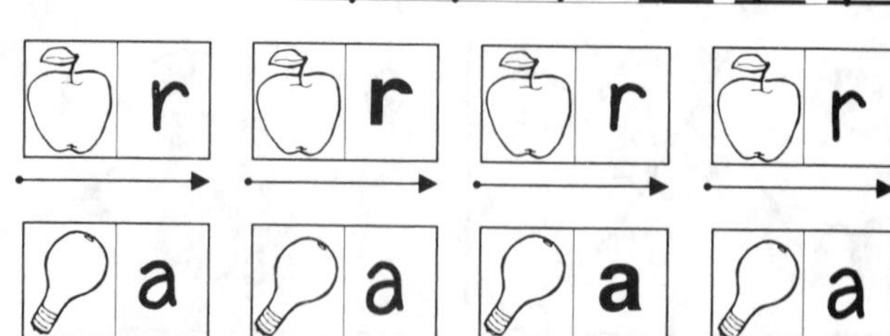

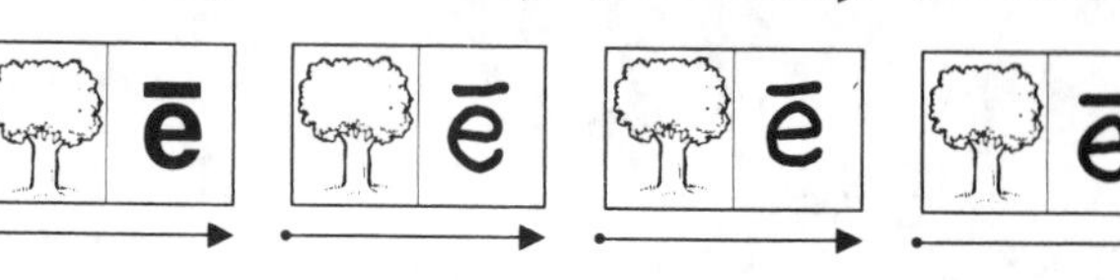

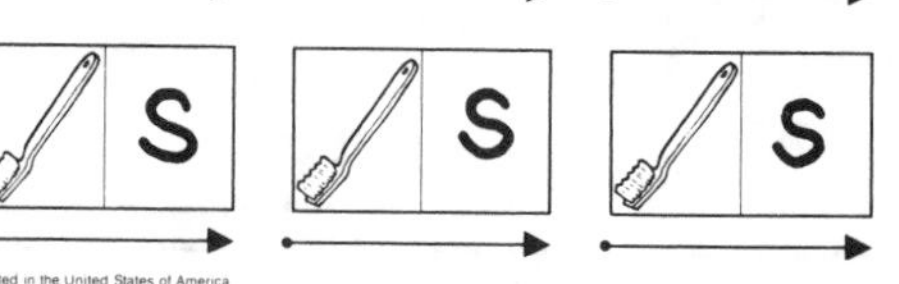

r r r r | a a a a | ē ē ē ē | s s s s

Printed in the United States of America

NAME ____________________

TAKE-HOME **32** SIDE **1**

m ē

s	r
r	a
f	s
a	f
m	ē
ē	m

f a r m a r ē

TAKE-HOME **32** SIDE 2

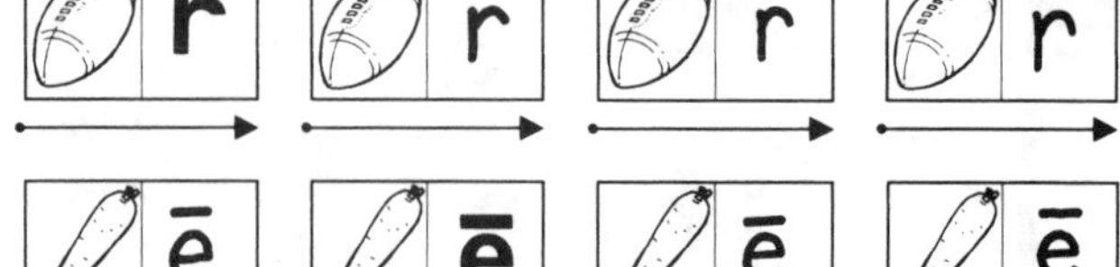

r r r r | ē ē ē ē

r r r r | d d d d

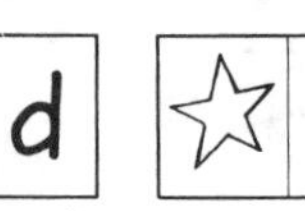

Printed in the United States of America

NAME

TAKE-HOME 33 SIDE 1

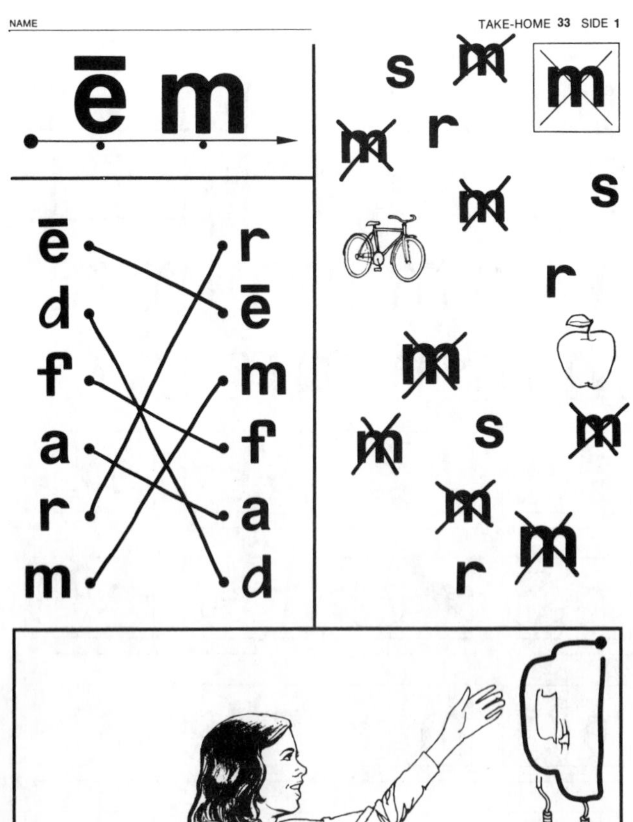

TAKE-HOME 33 SIDE 2

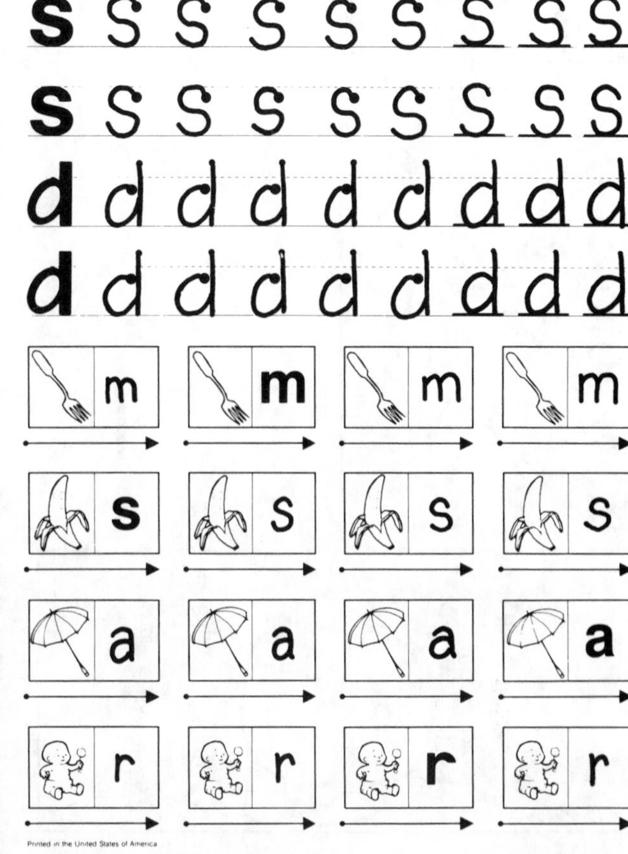

Printed in the United States of America

NAME

TAKE-HOME 34 SIDE 1

TAKE-HOME 34 SIDE 2

Printed in the United States of America

NAME

TAKE-HOME 35 SIDE 1

mē

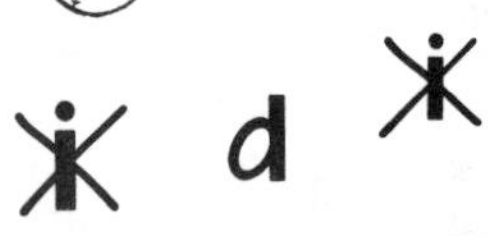

ē m s f a d

a f m d ē s

d f d s d f

TAKE-HOME 35 SIDE 2

i i i i i i i i i

i i i i i i i i i

m m m m m m m

m m m m m m m

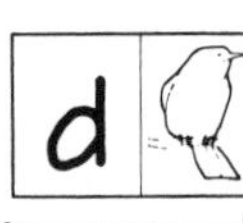

Printed in the United States of America

NAME

TAKE-HOME 36 SIDE 1

ēar

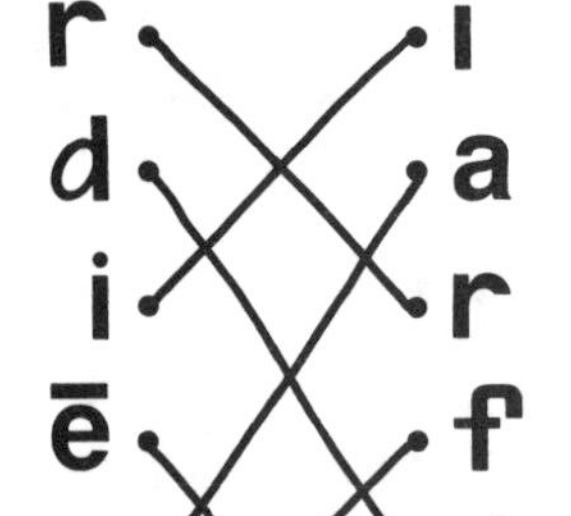

r d i ē a f

i a r f d ē

m ē i s i s

TAKE-HOME 36 SIDE 2

f f f f f f f f f

f f f f f f f f f

s s s s s s s s s

s s s s s s s s s

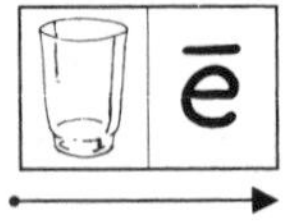
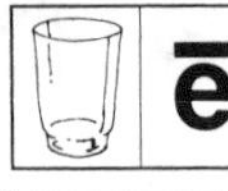

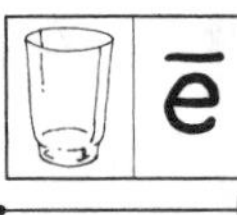

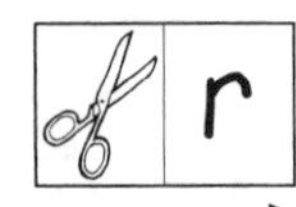

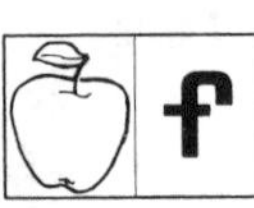

Printed in the United States of America

NAME

TAKE-HOME 37 SIDE 1

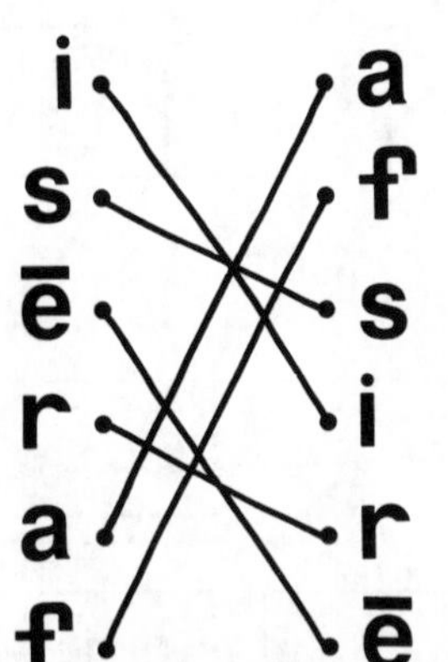

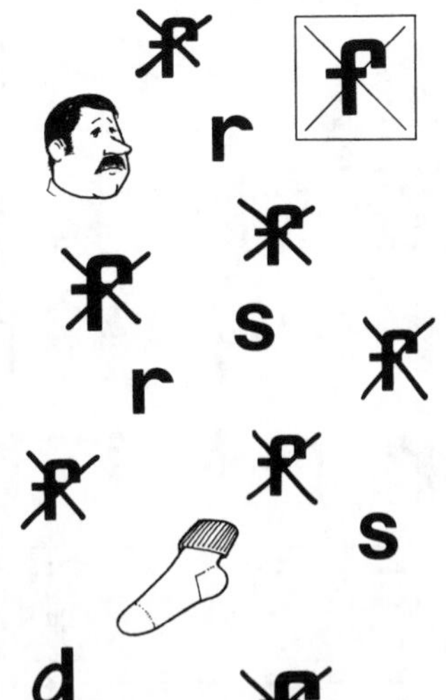

TAKE-HOME 37 SIDE 2

r r r r r r r r r

r r r r r r r r r

f f f f f f f f f

f f f f f f f f f

a a a a

ē ē ē ē

f f f f

d d d d

Printed in the United States of America

19

NAME

TAKE-HOME 38 SIDE 1

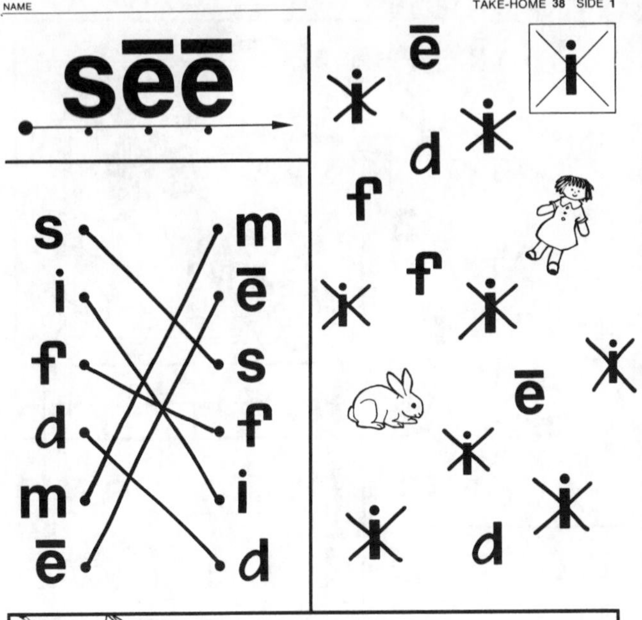

TAKE-HOME 38 SIDE 2

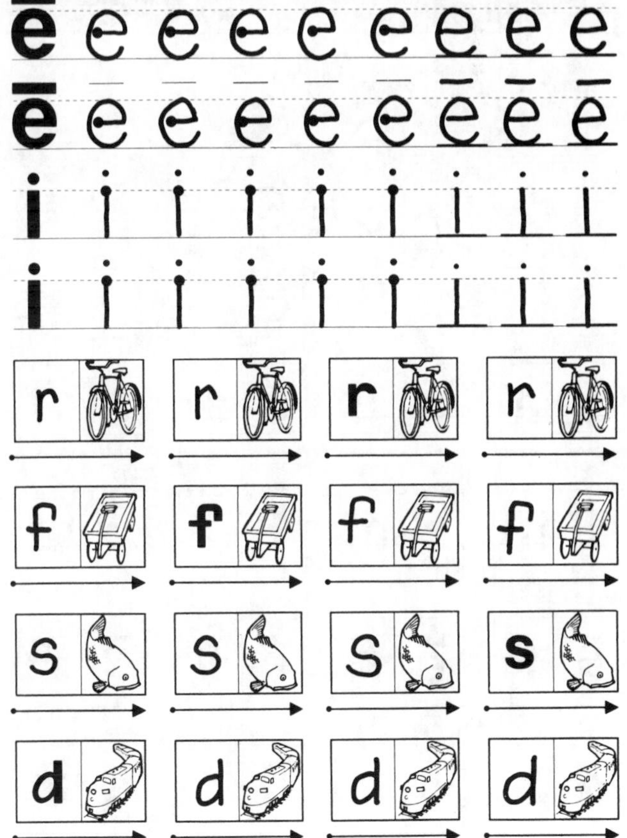

TAKE-HOME 39 SIDE 1

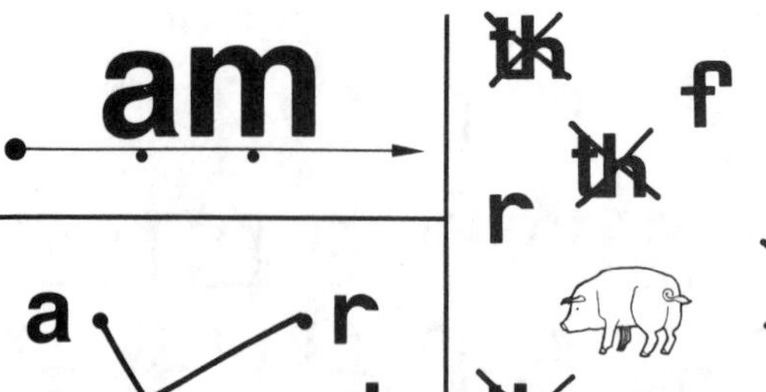

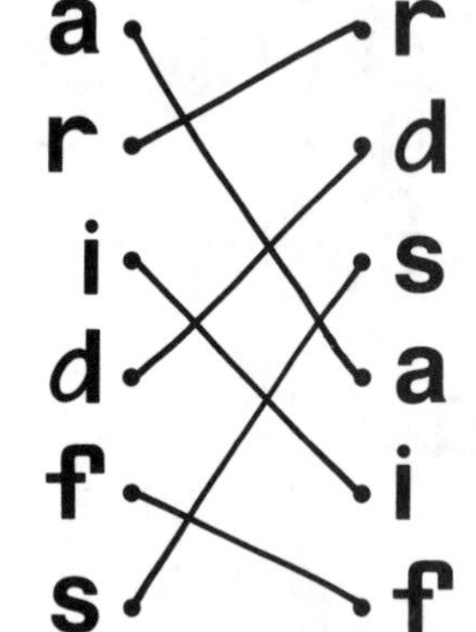

TAKE-HOME 39 SIDE 2

th th th th th th th

th th th th th th th

r r r r r r r r r

r r r r r r r r r

ē 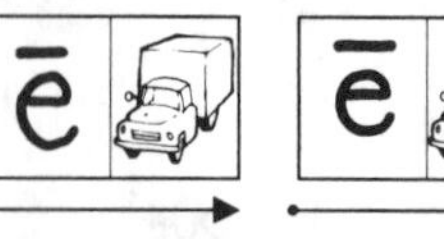 ē  ē  ē 

s  s  s  s 

i 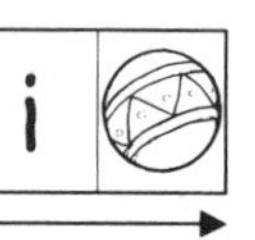 i 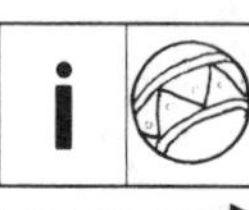 i  i 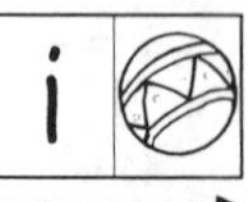

d  d  d  d 

Printed in the United States of America

NAME

TAKE-HOME 40 SIDE 1

am sēē

see

see

see

s	a	s	a	s	a	s	a
f	m	f	m	f	m	f	m
ē	f	ē	f	ē	f	ē	f
d	r	d	r	d	r	d	r

TAKE-HOME 40 SIDE 2

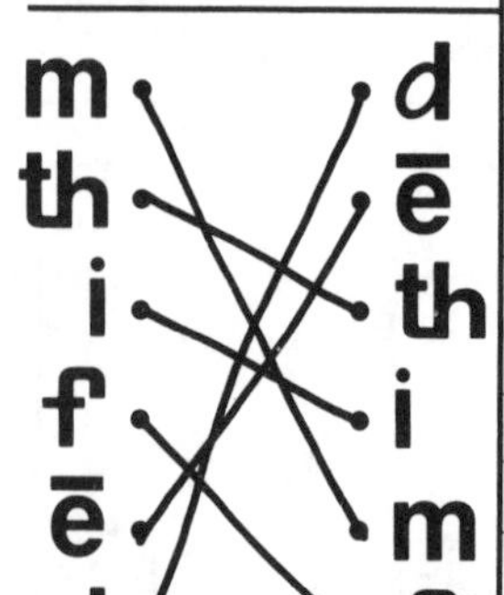

th th th th

th th th th

i i i i i i

a a a a a a

s s s s s s

d d d d d d

ē ē ē ē ē ē

Printed in the United States of America

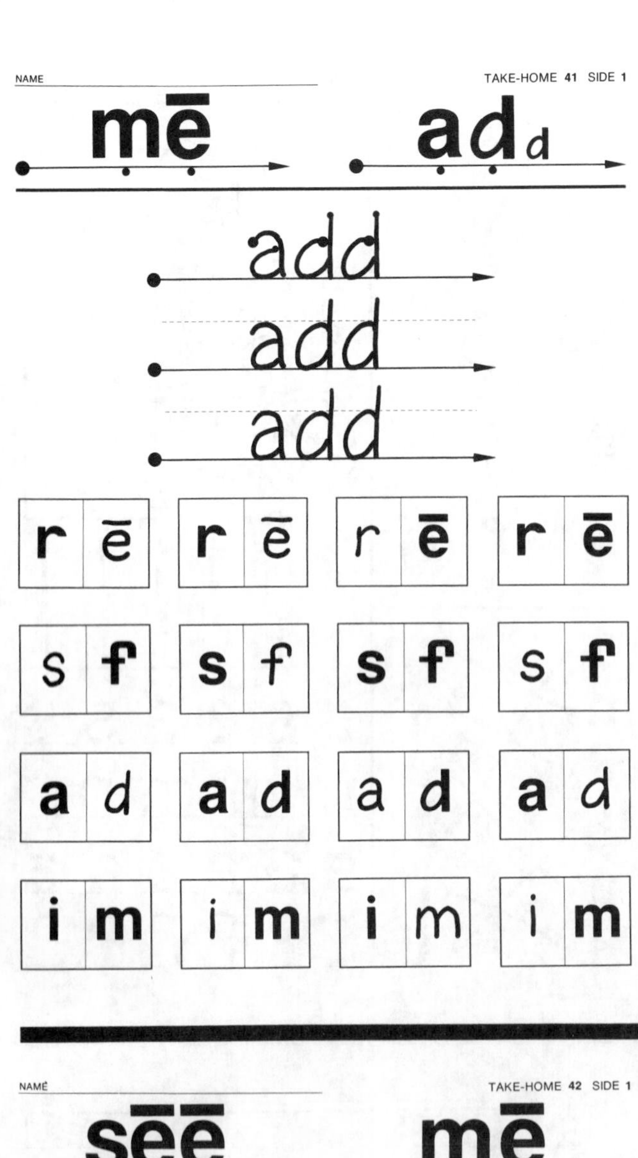
NAME
TAKE-HOME 41 SIDE 1
mē
add
add
add
add
r ē r ē r ē r ē
s f s f s f s f
a d a d a d a d
i m i m i m i m

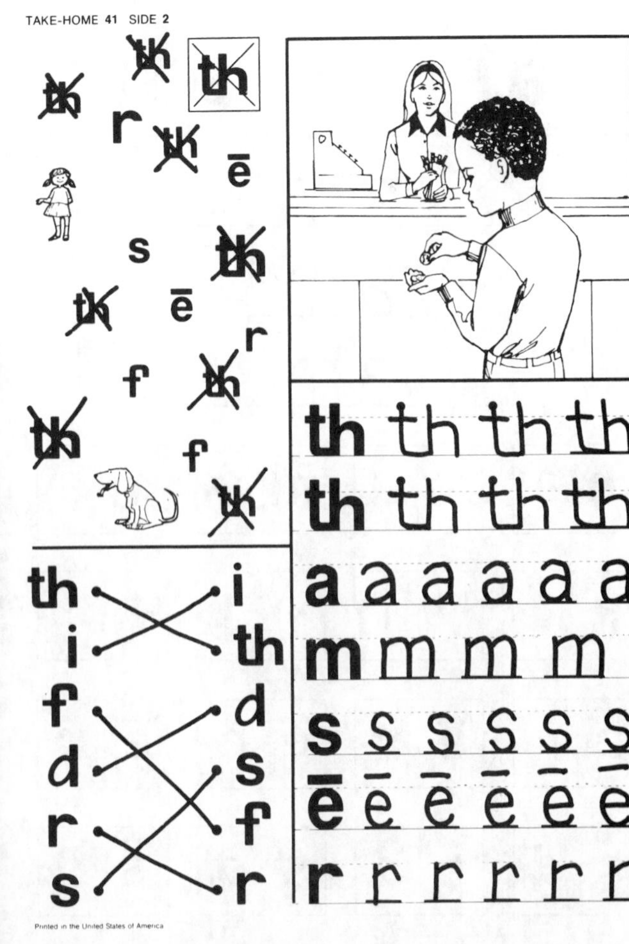
TAKE-HOME 41 SIDE 2
th r ē s ē r f f
th i
i th
f d
d s
r f
s r
th th th th
th th th th
a a a a a a
m m m m m
s s s s s s
ē ē ē ē ē ē
r r r r r r
Printed in the United States of America

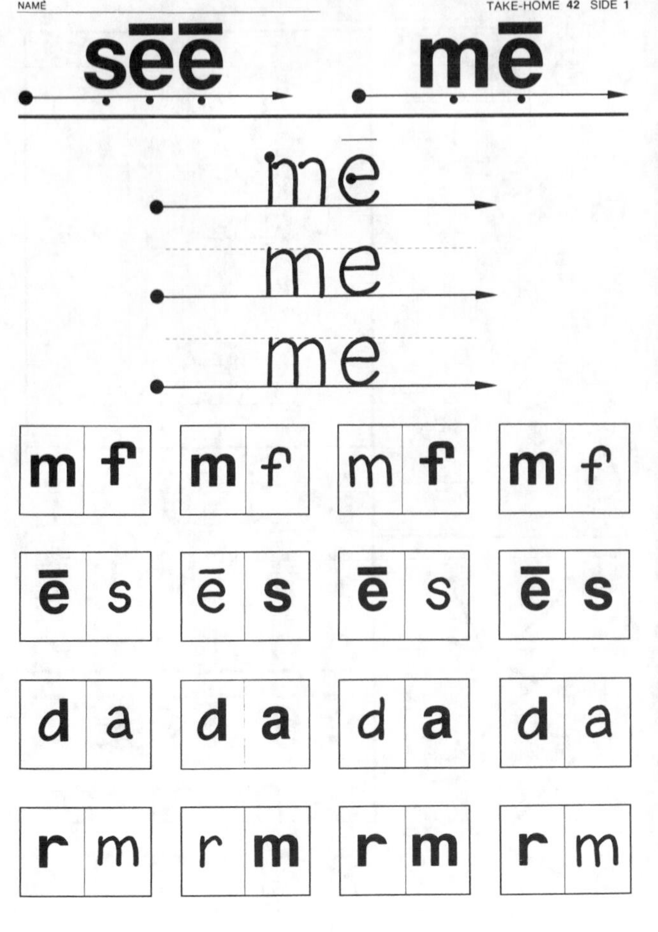
NAME
TAKE-HOME 42 SIDE 1
sēē
mē
mē
me
me
m f m f m f m f
ē s ē s ē s ē s
d a d a d a d a
r m r m r m r m

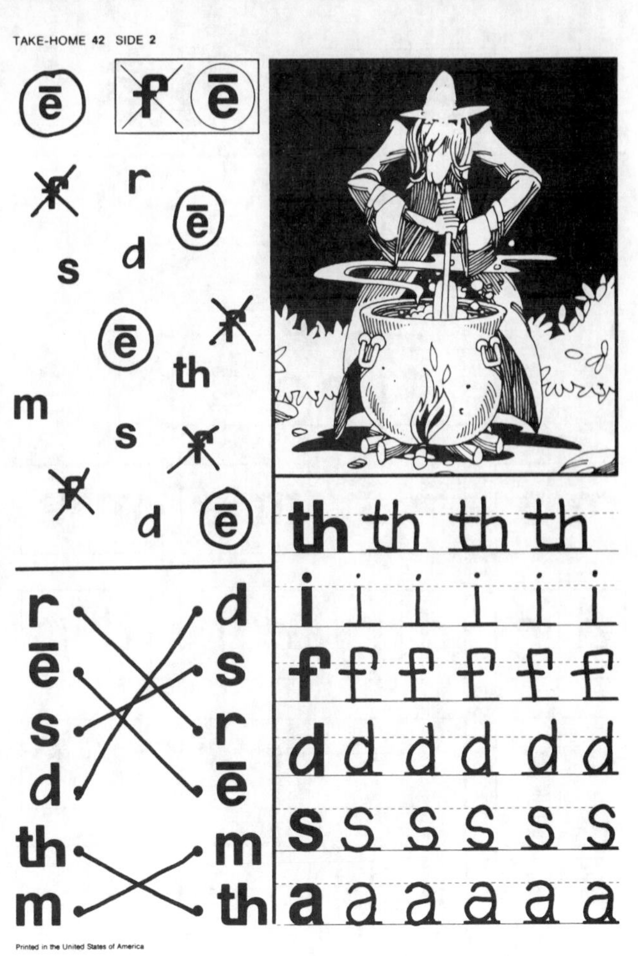
TAKE-HOME 42 SIDE 2
ē f ē r ē s d ē th m s d ē
r d
ē s
s r
d ē
th m
m th
th th th th
i i i i i i
f f f f f f
d d d d d d
s s s s s s
a a a a a a
Printed in the United States of America

22

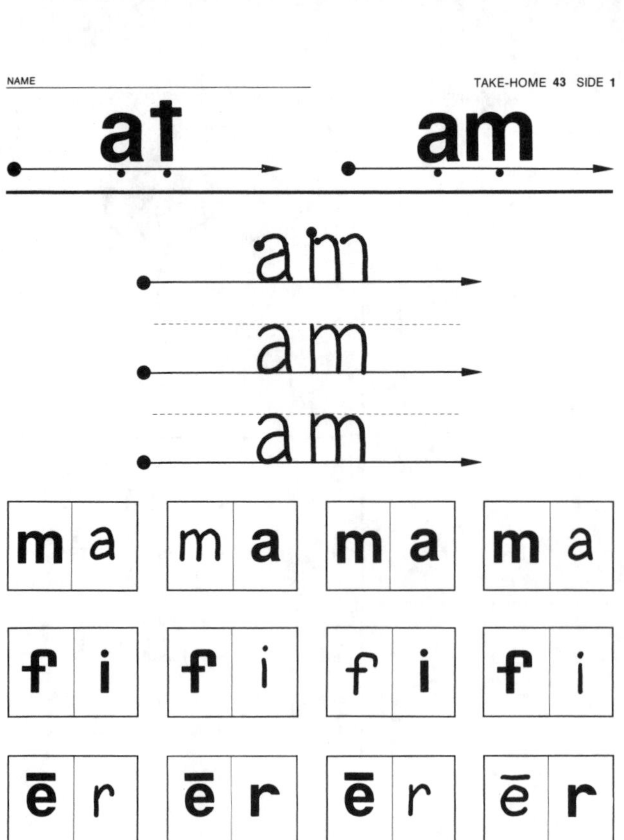

NAME

TAKE-HOME 43 SIDE 1

at am

am

am

am

m a	m a	m a	m a
f i	f i	f i	f i
ē r	ē r	ē r	ē r
s d	s d	s d	s d

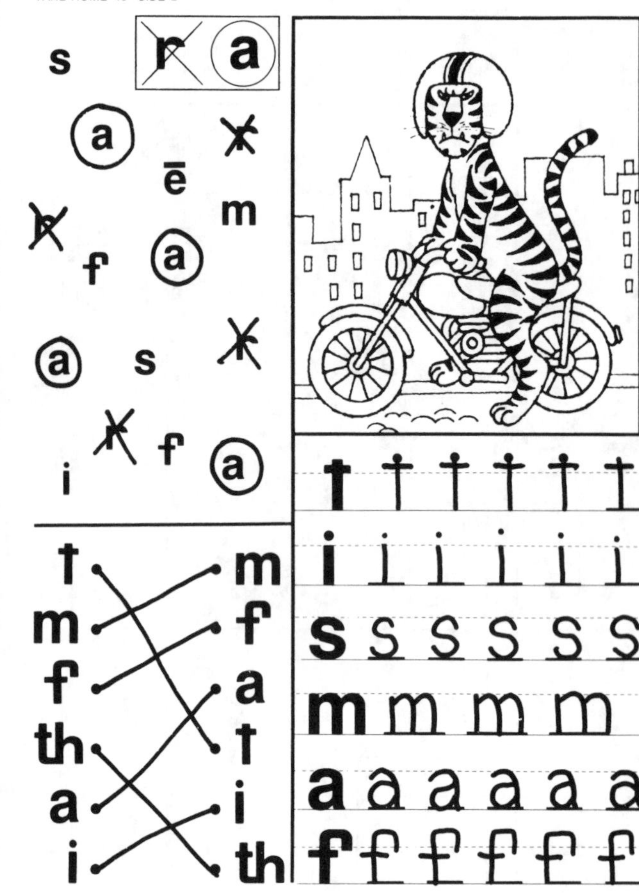

TAKE-HOME 43 SIDE 2

s r a

a ē m f a a s i f a

t m f th a i

m f a t i th

t t t t t t

i i i i i i

s s s s s s

m m m m

a a a a a a

f f f f f f

Printed in the United States of America

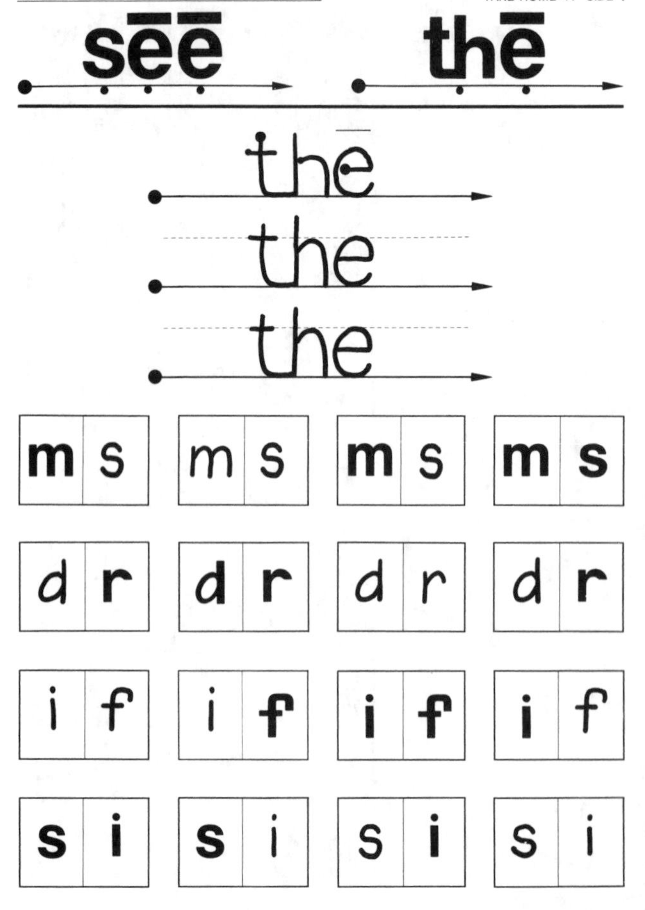

NAME

TAKE-HOME 44 SIDE 1

sēē thē

the

the

the

m s	m s	m s	m s
d r	d r	d r	d r
i f	i f	i f	i f
s i	s i	s i	s i

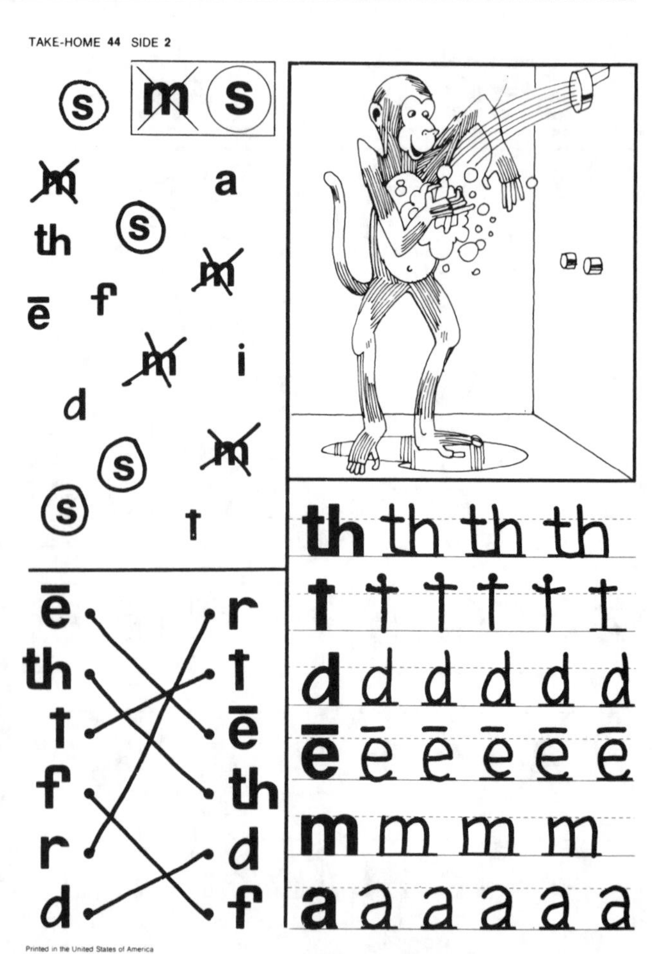

TAKE-HOME 44 SIDE 2

s m s

a th s ē f i d s s t

ē th t f r d

r t ē th d f

th th th th

t t t t t t

d d d d d d

ē ē ē ē ē ē

m m m m

a a a a a a

Printed in the United States of America

NAME ______________________

TAKE-HOME 45 SIDE 1

mē ēat

me

me

me

ē d	ē d	ē d	ē d
i m	i m	i m	i m
a s	a s	a s	a s
r d	r d	r d	r d

TAKE-HOME 45 SIDE 2

th r

r i th r th m r th i f r d f th a

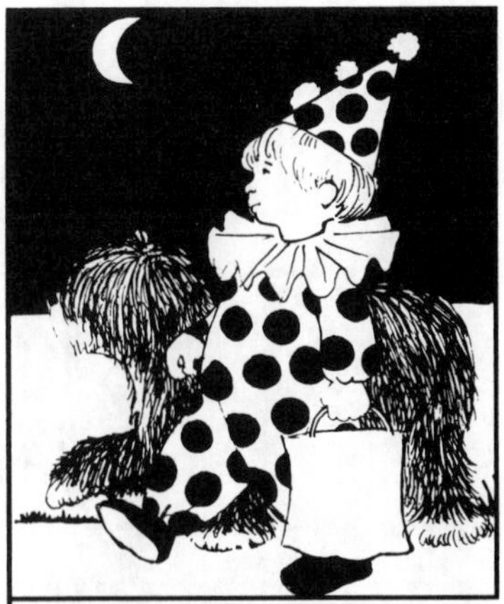

i	t
t	m
a	s
f	i
m	f
s	a

t t t t t t

i i i i i i

s s s s s s

d d d d d d

r r r r r r

ē ē ē ē ē ē

Printed in the United States of America

23

NAME ______________________

TAKE-HOME 46 SIDE 1

mad is

is

is

is

f m	f m	f m	f m
d a	d a	d a	d a
s f	s f	s f	s f
t ē	t ē	t ē	t ē

TAKE-HOME 46 SIDE 2

d m

n d m t r d ē m m th i d d f m

n	th
t	i
i	t
th	r
d	n
r	d

n n n n n n

f f f f f f

d d d d d d

t t t t t t

m m m m

a a a a a a

Printed in the United States of America

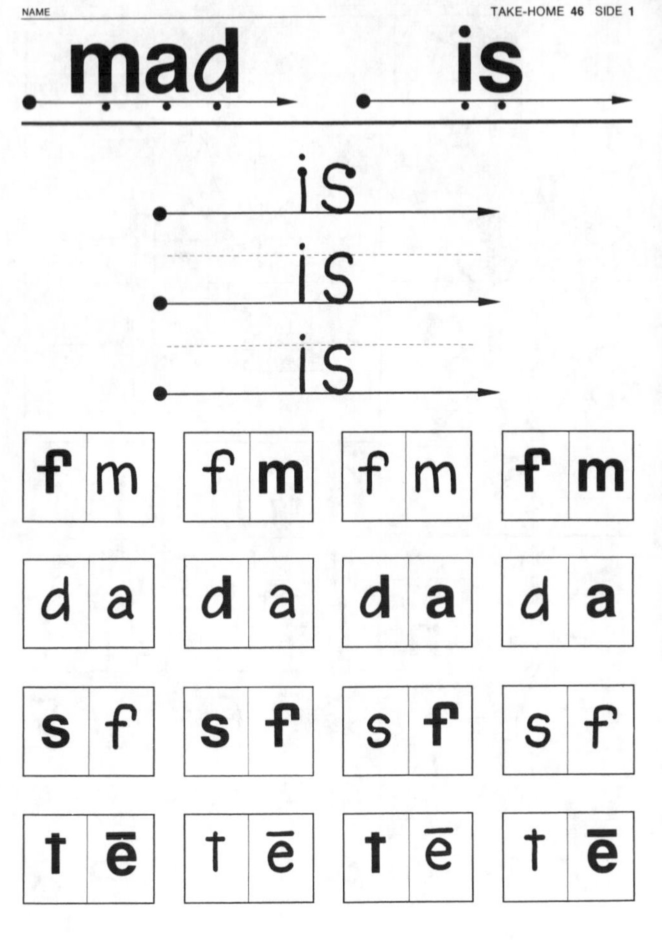

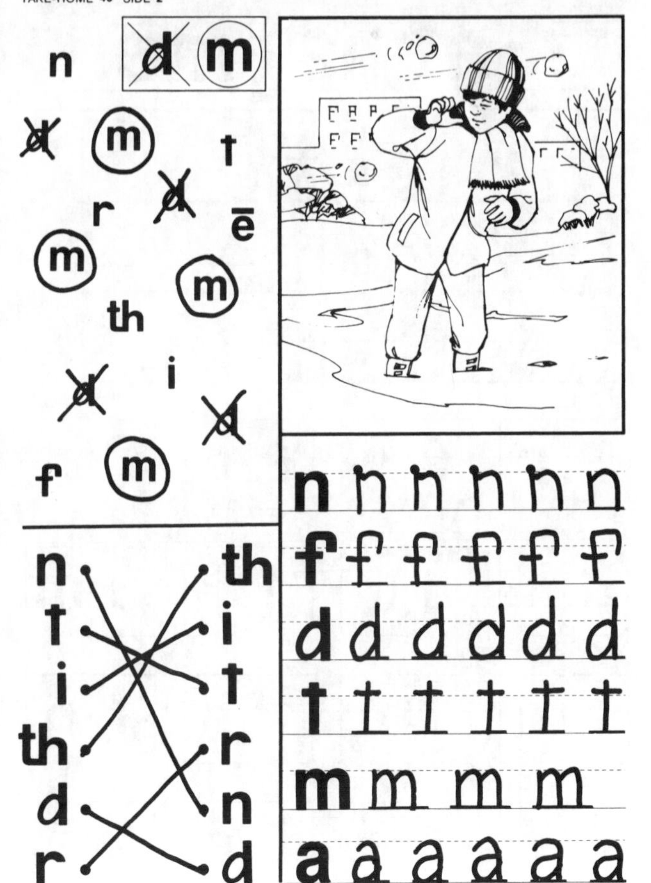

NAME ______________________ TAKE-HOME **47** SIDE **1**

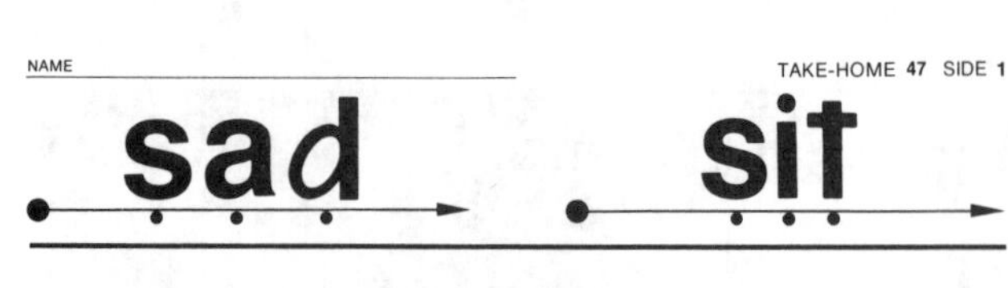

sit

sit

sit

r	t		r	t		r	t		r	t
a	f		a	f		a	f		a	f
m	i		m	i		m	i		m	i
s	ē		s	ē		s	ē		s	ē

TAKE-HOME **47** SIDE **2**

t	s
i	r
th	t
r	i
ē	th
s	ē

t t t t t t

a a a a a a

n n n n n n

m m m m

s s s s s s

ē ē ē ē ē ē

NAME ______________________ TAKE-HOME **48** SIDE **1**

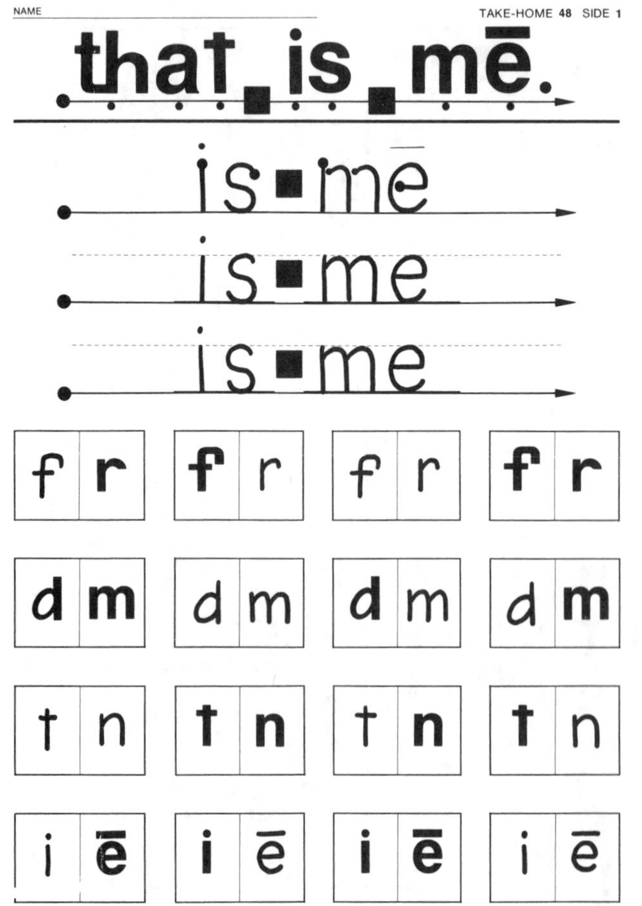

TAKE-HOME **48** SIDE **2**

NAME ________ TAKE-HOME 49 SIDE 1

sēē ■ mē ■ ēat.

see ■ me

see ■ me

see ■ me

n ē	n ē	n ē	n ē
r n	r n	r n	r n
i f	i f	i f	i f
d t	d t	d t	d t

TAKE-HOME 49 SIDE 2

f a

f t i a s f th a f a t n f a i

n r i th f m — m th r f i n

n n n n n n
t t t t t t
s s s s s s
m m m m
d d d d d d
r r r r r r

Printed in the United States of America

NAME ________ TAKE-HOME 50 SIDE 1

it ■ is ■ fat.

it ■ is ■ fat.

it ■ is ■ fat.

it ■ is ■ fat.

 a  f

 a 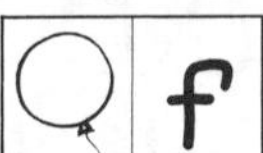 f 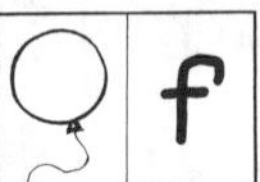 f  a

 f  a  a 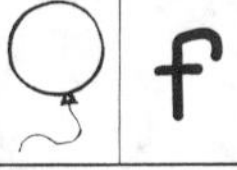 f

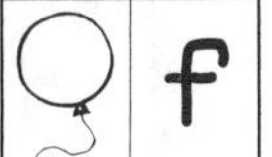 f  a 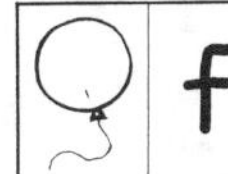 f  a

TAKE-HOME 50 SIDE 2

n i n

th i t c n i n d th f n i i c

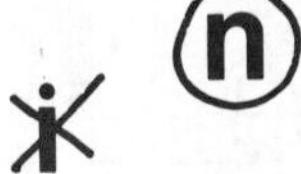

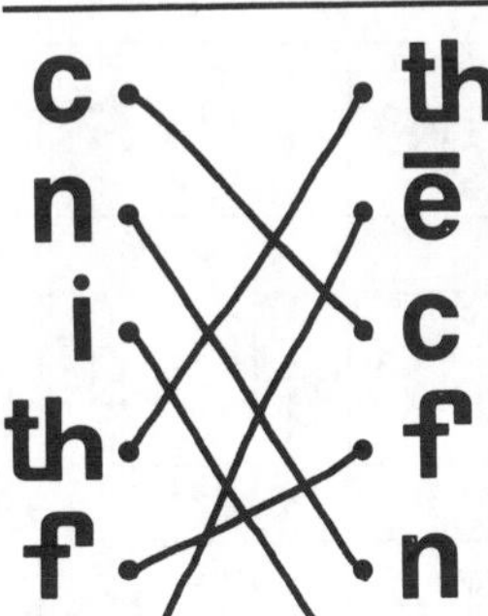

c n i th f ē — th ē c f n i

c c c c c c
t t t t t t
f f f f f f
n n n n n n
m m m m
i i i i i i

Printed in the United States of America

NAME

that fan ran.

that fan

that fan

that fan

 m  ē

 m  ē  m  m

 m  m  ē  ē

 ē  ē  ē  m

r ē

c i ē t ē r th r n ē t c ē r

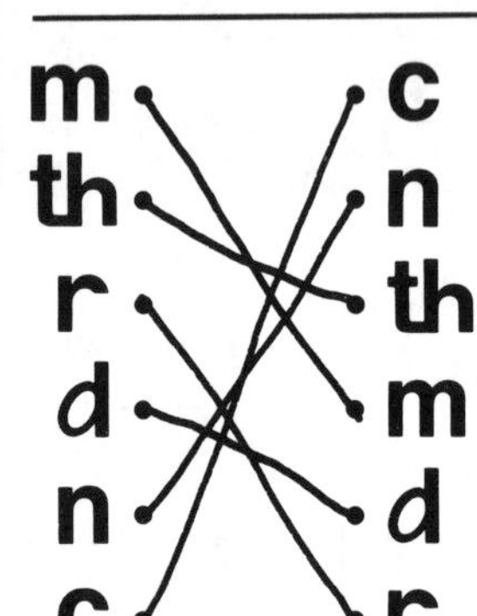

m th r d n c

c n th m d r

c c c c c c

d d d d d d

t t t t t t

o o o o o o

n n n n n n

ē ē ē ē ē ē

NAME

sēē mē sit.

sēē mē

sēē mē

sēē mē

 s  m

 s  m  m  s

 m  s  m  s

 s  m  s  m

c n

i t th c f c n n i c t n th n c

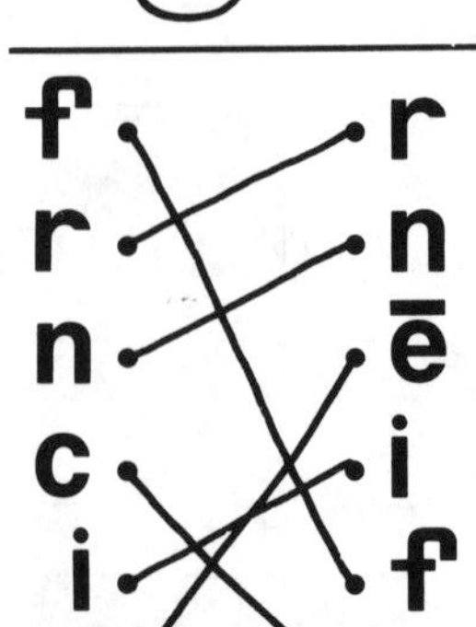

f r n c i ē

r n ē i f c

n n n n n n

c c c c c c

th th th th

t t t t t t

i i i i i i

d d d d d d

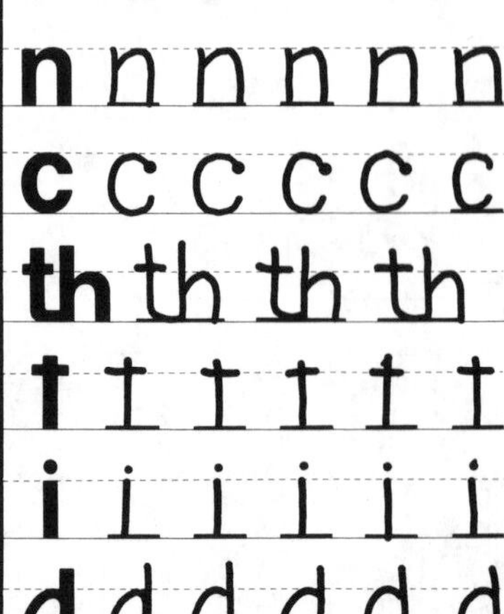

NAME TAKE-HOME 53 SIDE 1

thē sad man

sad man

sad man

sad man

 a
 ē

 ē a
 a
 ē

 a
 ē
 ē
 a

 a
 a
 ē
 ē

TAKE-HOME 53 SIDE 2

n f c

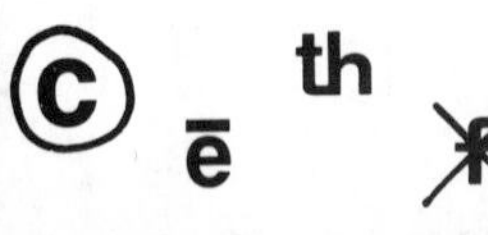

n c t d f c c i f c th ē f

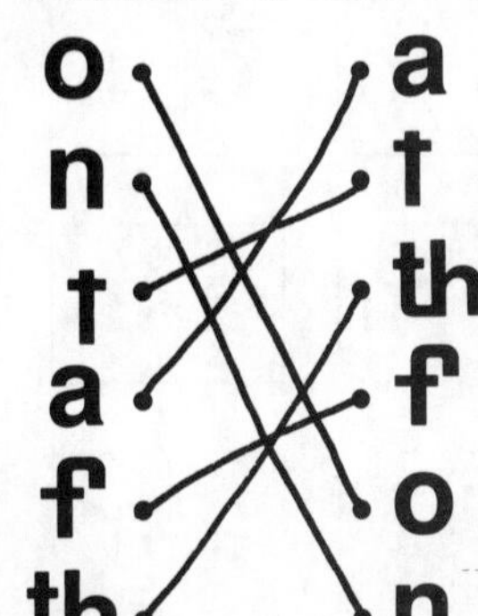

o n t a f th — a t th f o n

n n n n n n

o o o o o o

m m m m

t t t t t t

ē ē ē ē ē ē

r r r r r r

Printed in the United States of America

NAME TAKE-HOME 54 SIDE 1

mad at mē

at mē

at me

at me

 f
 d

 f d
 f d

d d f f

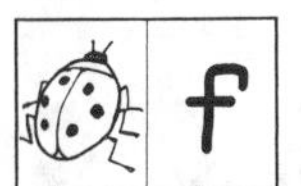 f
 f
 d
 d

TAKE-HOME 54 SIDE 2

c t i

t i f i ē t n t i i c th t n

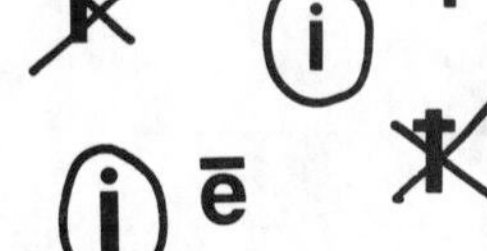

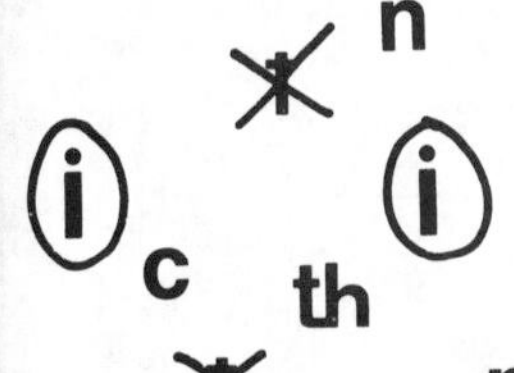

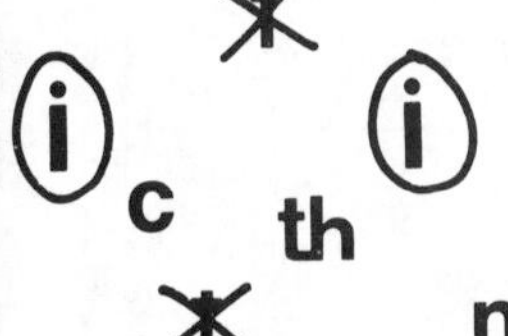

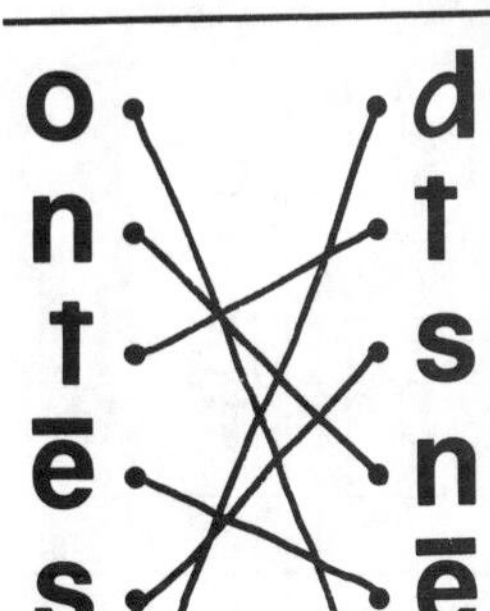

o n t ē s d — d t s n ē o

c c c c c c

o o o o o o

n n n n n n

t t t t t t

s s s s s s

a a a a a a

Printed in the United States of America

NAME ______ TAKE-HOME 55 SIDE 1

thē fat rat

the fat rat

the fat rat

the fat rat

a	m

ē	i

a m	ē i	a m	ē i
ē i	ē i	a m	a m
a m	ē i	ē i	a m

TAKE-HOME 55 SIDE 2

o	d

o d th c d o t f d n th o d d c o

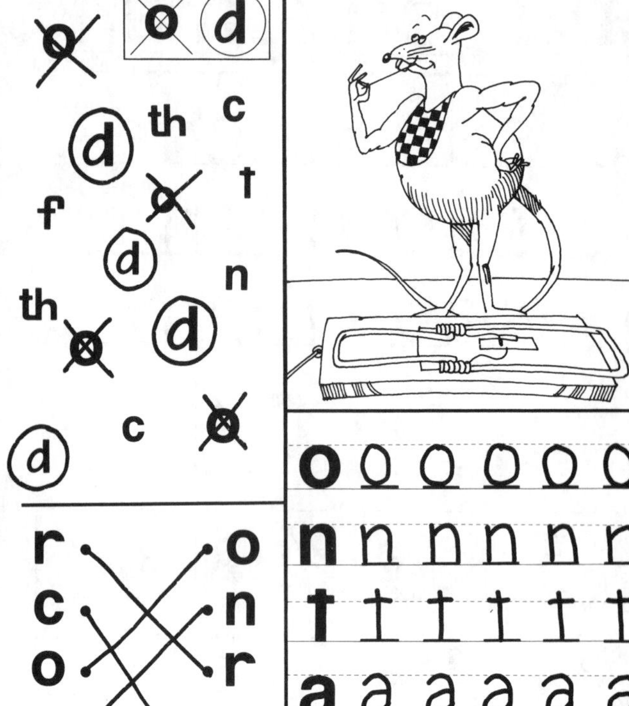

o o o o o o

n n n n n n

t t t t t t

a a a a a a

c c c c c c

r r r r r r

r	o
c	n
o	r
n	m
th	c
m	th

Printed in the United States of America

NAME ______ TAKE-HOME 56 SIDE 1

not a rock.

a rock

a rock

a rock

d	s

f	r

d s	f r	f r	d s
f r	d s	d s	f r
d s	f r	f r	d s

TAKE-HOME 56 SIDE 2

r	m

n m r o r th t m r o r t m c m

c c c c c c

n n n n n n

o o o o o o

m m m m

a a a a a a

d d d d d d

n	c
th	ē
t	a
ē	t
c	n
a	th

Printed in the United States of America

NAME

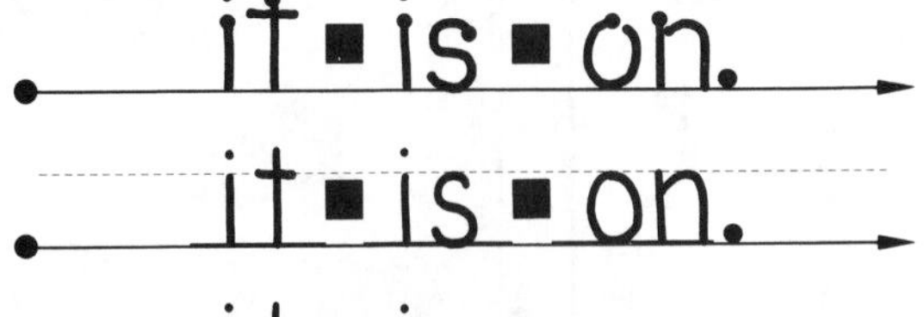

ē	n

c	o

c o	ē n	c o	c o
ē n	c o	ē n	ē n
c o	ē n	c o	ē n

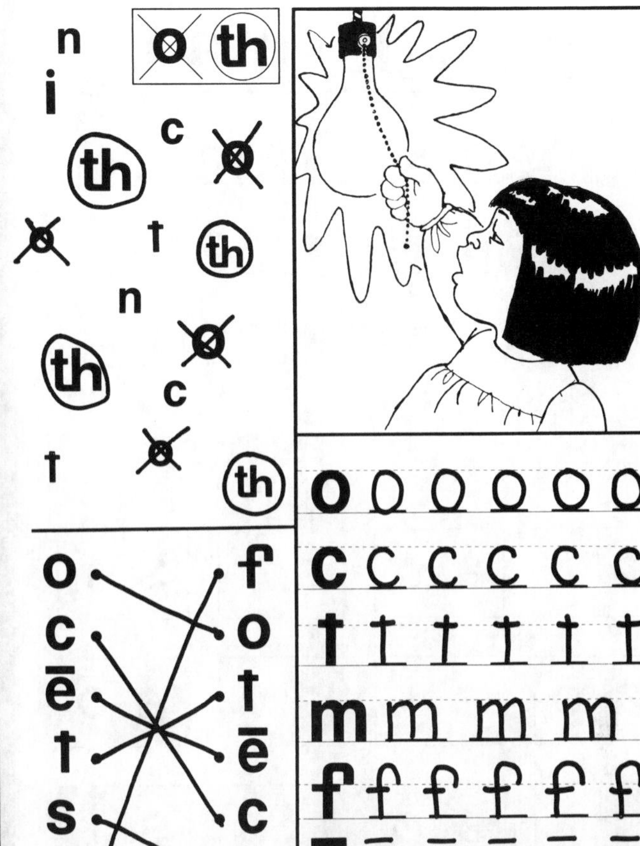

Printed in the United States of America

NAME

sit ▪ on ▪ it.

sit ▪ on ▪ it.

sit ▪ on ▪ it.

sit ▪ on ▪ it.

t	f

r	th

t f	t f	r th	t f
r th	r th	t f	r th
t f	r th	r th	t f

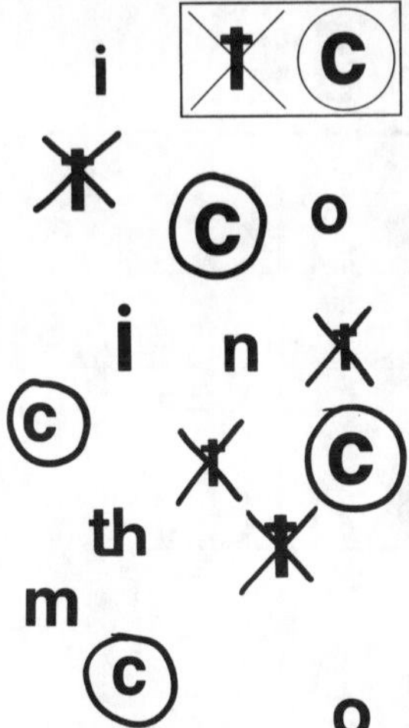

n n n n n n

t t t t t t

c c c c c c

i i i i i i

th th th th

r r r r r r

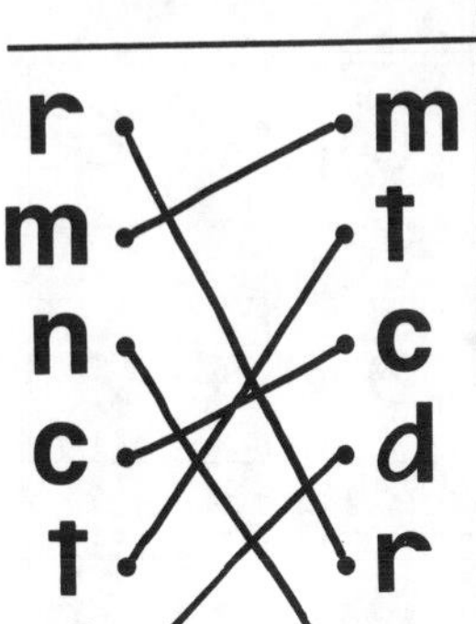

Printed in the United States of America

NAME

TAKE-HOME **59** SIDE **1**

sam■is■mad.

sam■is■mad.

sam■is■mad.

sam■is■mad.

s	i		a	o

s i	a o	s i	s i
a o	s i	a o	a o
s i	a o	a o	s i

TAKE-HOME **59** SIDE **2**

n r n

r ā r th n t n r th c r t n i

a a a a a a

m m m m

o o o o o o

t t t t t t

s s s s s s

ē ē ē ē ē ē

c	d
d	f
s	ē
o	s
ē	o
f	c

Printed in the United States of America.

NAME

TAKE-HOME **60** SIDE **1**

thē■rat■āte.

thē■rat■āte.

the■rat■ate.

the■rat■ate.

ē	ā		t	th

t th	ē ā	t th	t th
ē ā	t th	ē ā	ē ā
t th	ē ā	t th	ē ā

TAKE-HOME **60** SIDE **2**

c n a

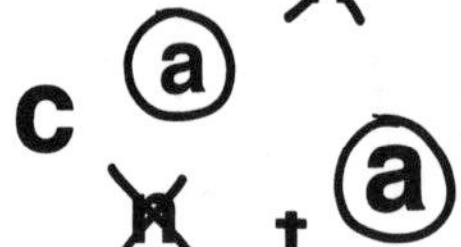

a a a a a a

o o o o o o

n n n n n n

c c c c c c

th th th th

s s s s s s

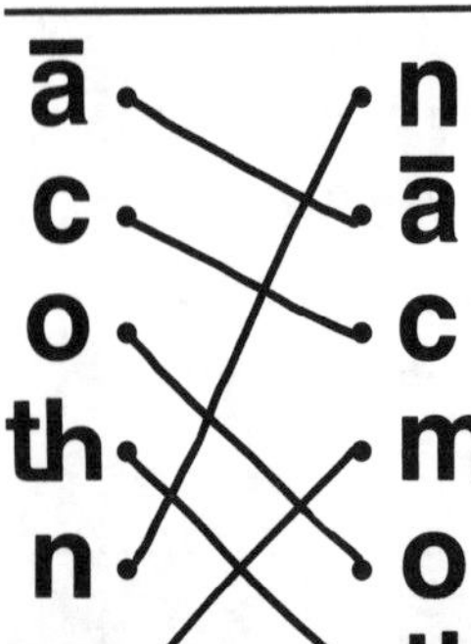

Printed in the United States of America

NAME ______________________ TAKE-HOME 61 SIDE 1

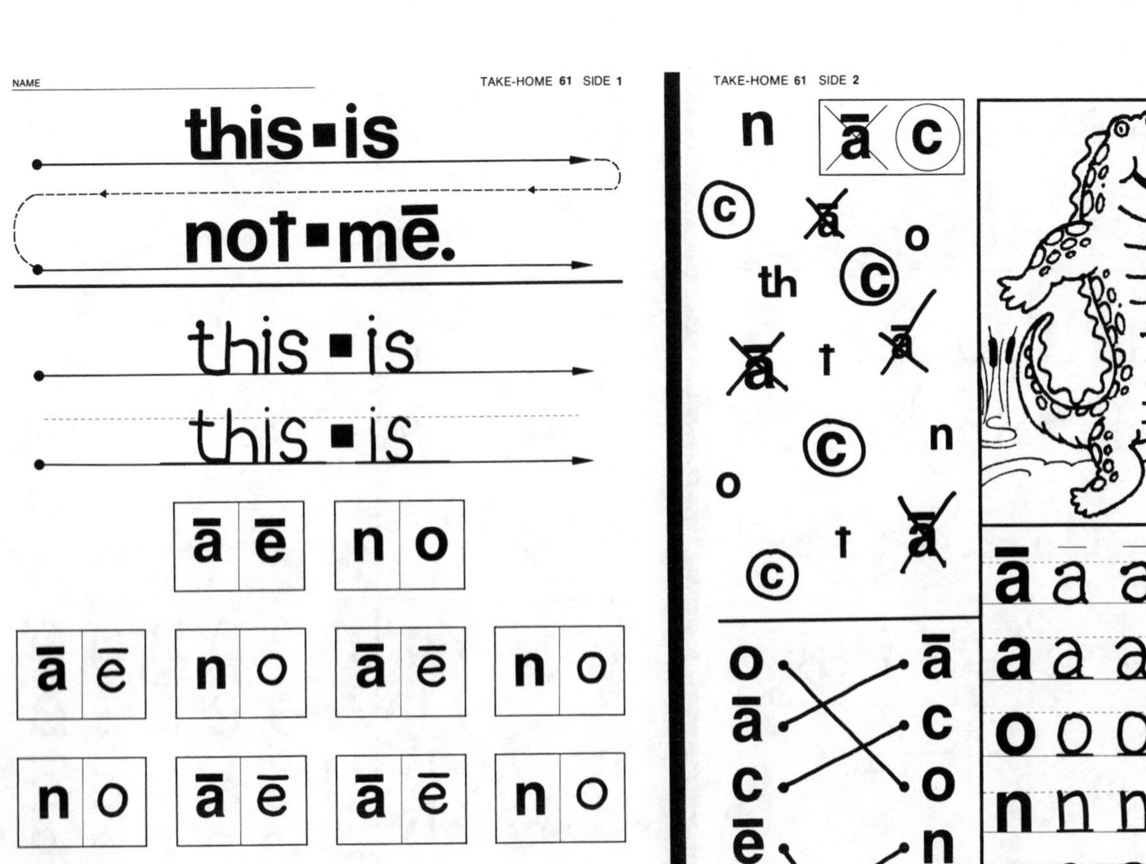

this ■ is
not ■ mē.

this ■ is

this ■ is

ā	ē

n	o

ā ē	n o	ā ē	n o
n o	ā ē	ā ē	n o
ā ē	n o	n o	ā ē

TAKE-HOME 61 SIDE 2

n ā c

c ā o th c ā t ā c n o t ā c

o ā c ē n th — ā c o n th ē

ā a a a a ā
a a a a a a
o o o o o o
n n n n n n
s s s s s s
ē ē ē ē ē ē

Printed in the United States of America

NAME ______________________ TAKE-HOME 62 SIDE 1

this ■ is
a ■ rock.

this ■ is

this ■ is

o	c

f	n

f n	o c	o c	f n
f n	f n	o c	o c
o c	o c	f n	f n

TAKE-HOME 62 SIDE 2

f t f

c t t f n o th t f th c f t o

307

ā o m c s t — s m ā o t c

a a a a a a
c c c c c c
o o o o o o
ā a a a a ā
i i i i i i
ē ē ē ē ē ē

Printed in the United States of America

32

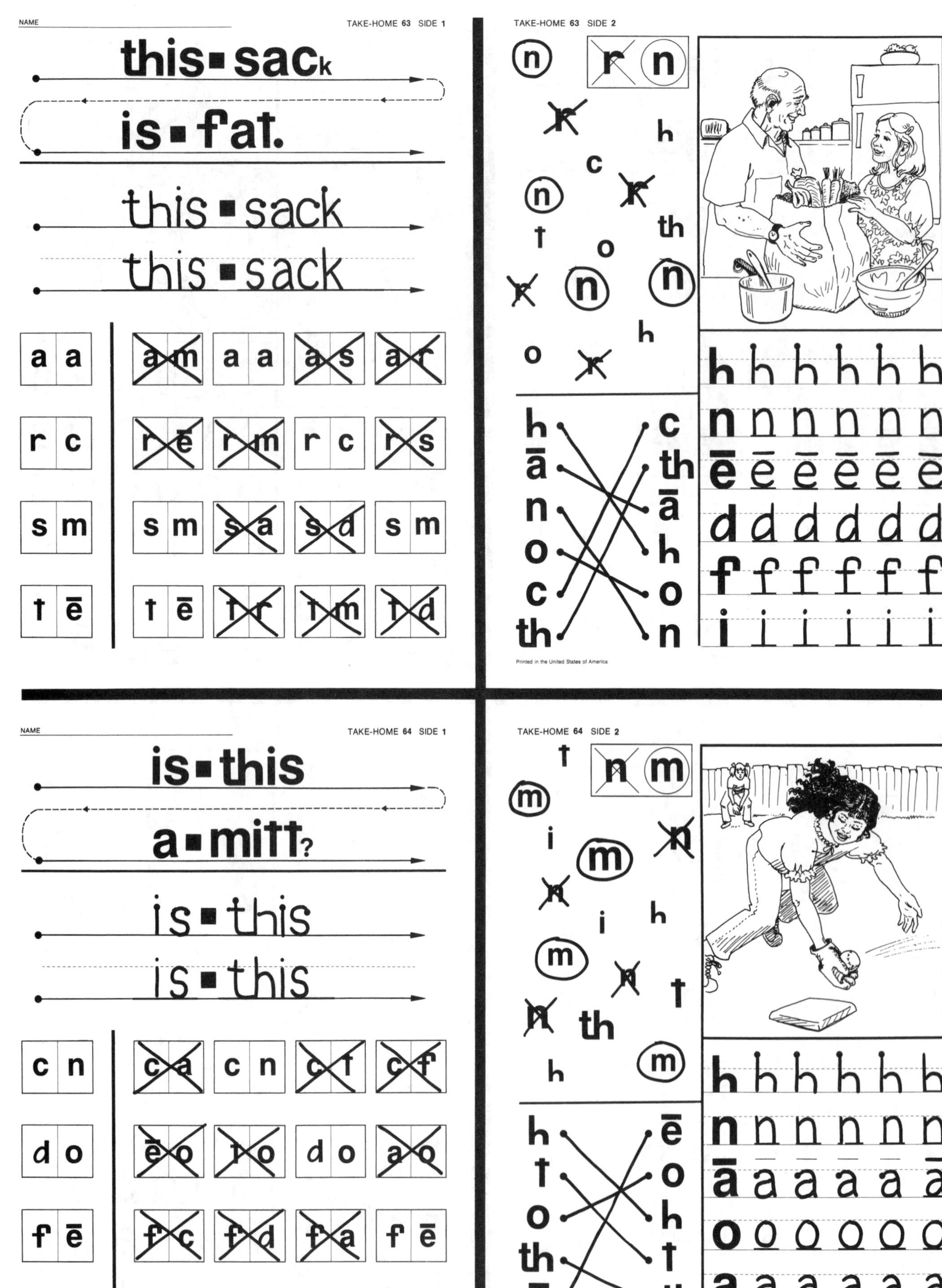
NAME
TAKE-HOME 63 SIDE 1
this sack
is fat.
this sack
this sack
TAKE-HOME 63 SIDE 2
Printed in the United States of America
NAME
TAKE-HOME 64 SIDE 1
is this
a mitt?
is this
is this
TAKE-HOME 64 SIDE 2
Printed in the United States of America

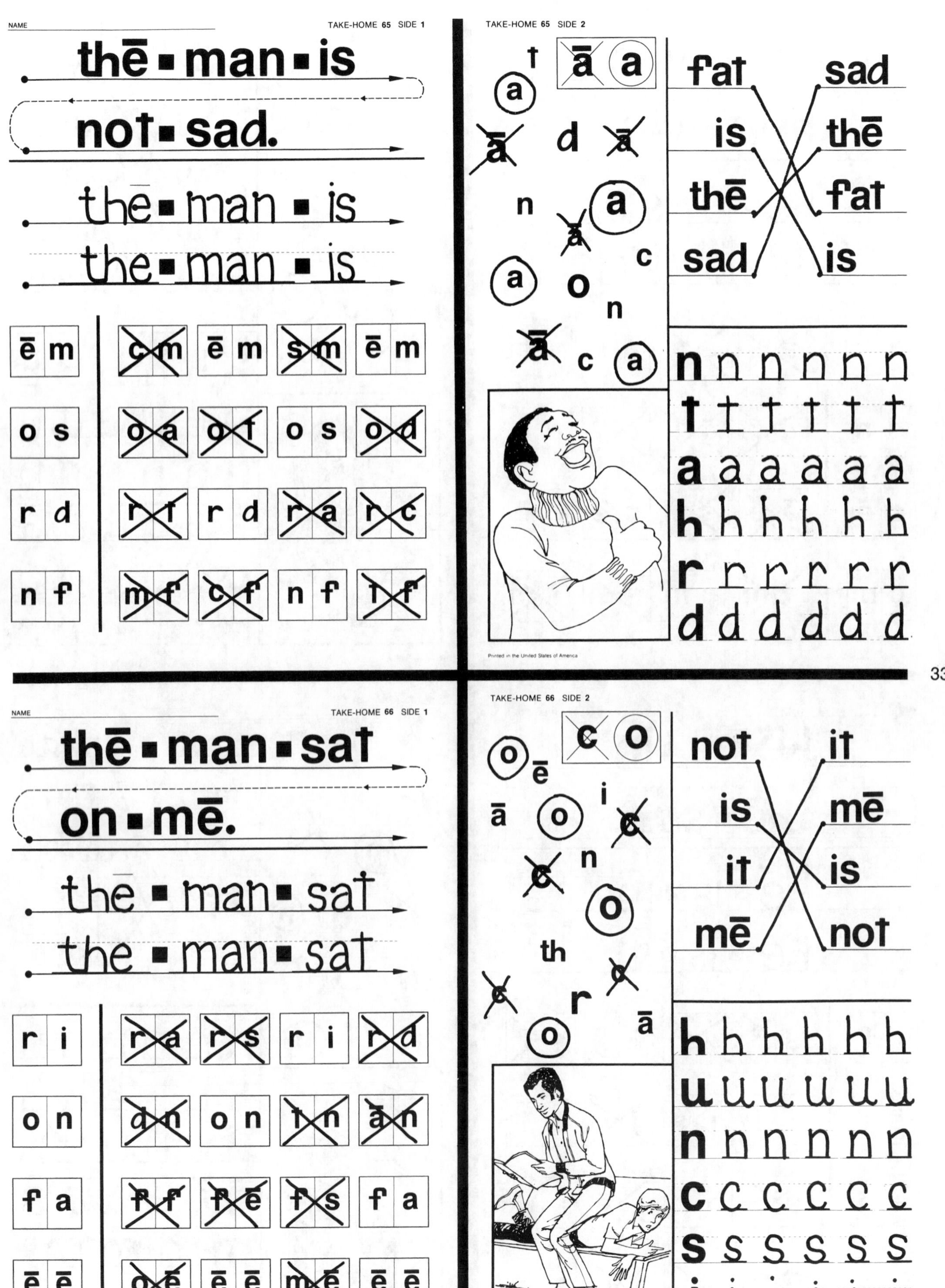
NAME
TAKE-HOME 65 SIDE 1
thē ▪ man ▪ is
not ▪ sad.
thē ▪ man ▪ is
the ▪ man ▪ is
ē m
o s
r d
n f
TAKE-HOME 65 SIDE 2
fat
is
thē
sad
sad
thē
fat
is
n n n n n n
t t t t t t
a a a a a a
h h h h h h
r r r r r r
d d d d d d
Printed in the United States of America
NAME
TAKE-HOME 66 SIDE 1
thē ▪ man ▪ sat
on ▪ mē.
thē ▪ man ▪ sat
the ▪ man ▪ sat
r i
o n
f a
ē ē
TAKE-HOME 66 SIDE 2
not
is
it
mē
it
mē
is
not
h h h h h h
u u u u u u
n n n n n n
c c c c c c
s s s s s s
i i i i i i
Printed in the United States of America

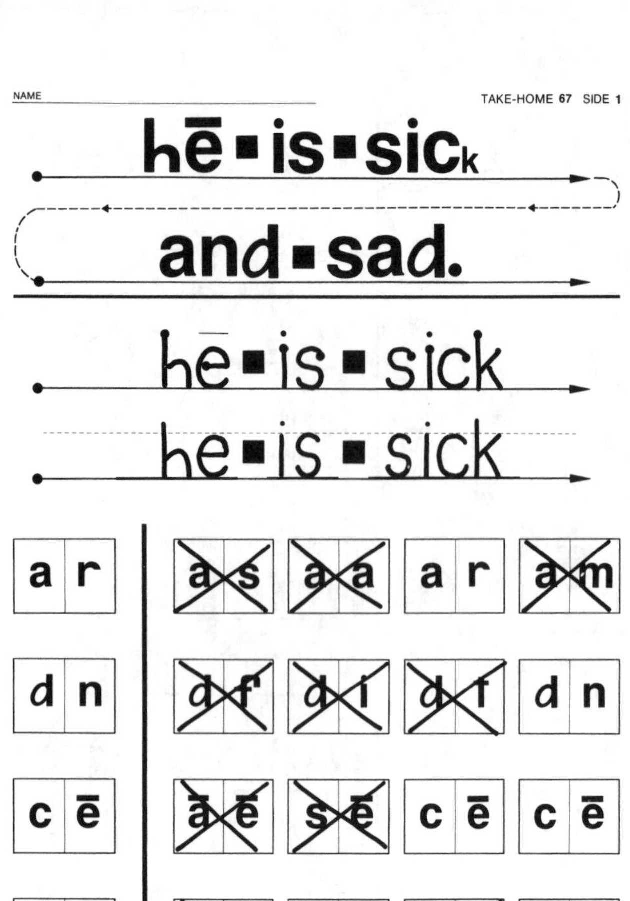
NAME
TAKE-HOME 67 SIDE 1
hē is sick
and sad.
hē is sick
he is sick

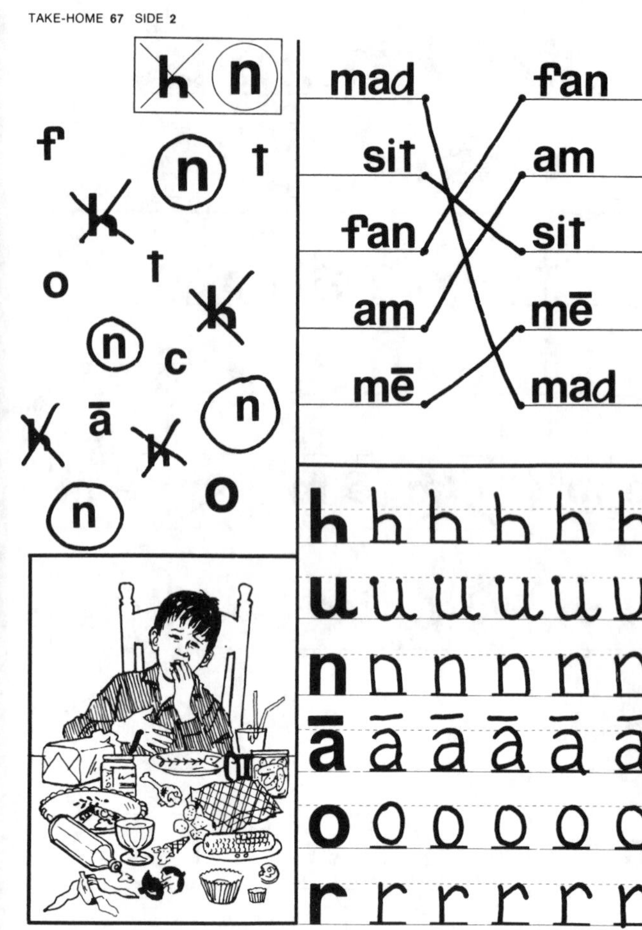
TAKE-HOME 67 SIDE 2
mad sit fan am mē
fan am sit mē mad
Printed in the United States of America

34

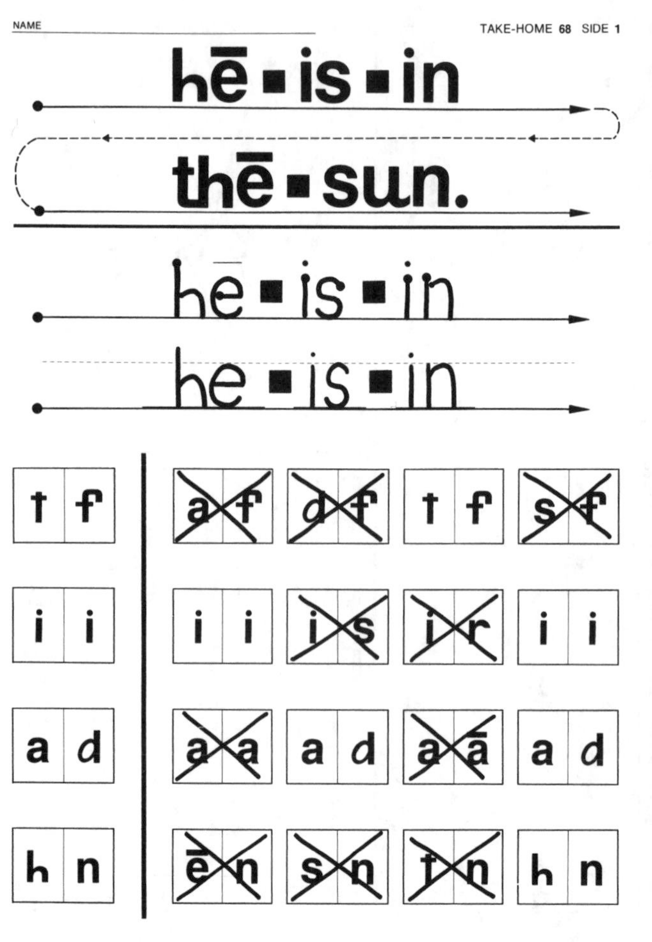
NAME
TAKE-HOME 68 SIDE 1
hē is in
thē sun.
hē is in
he is in

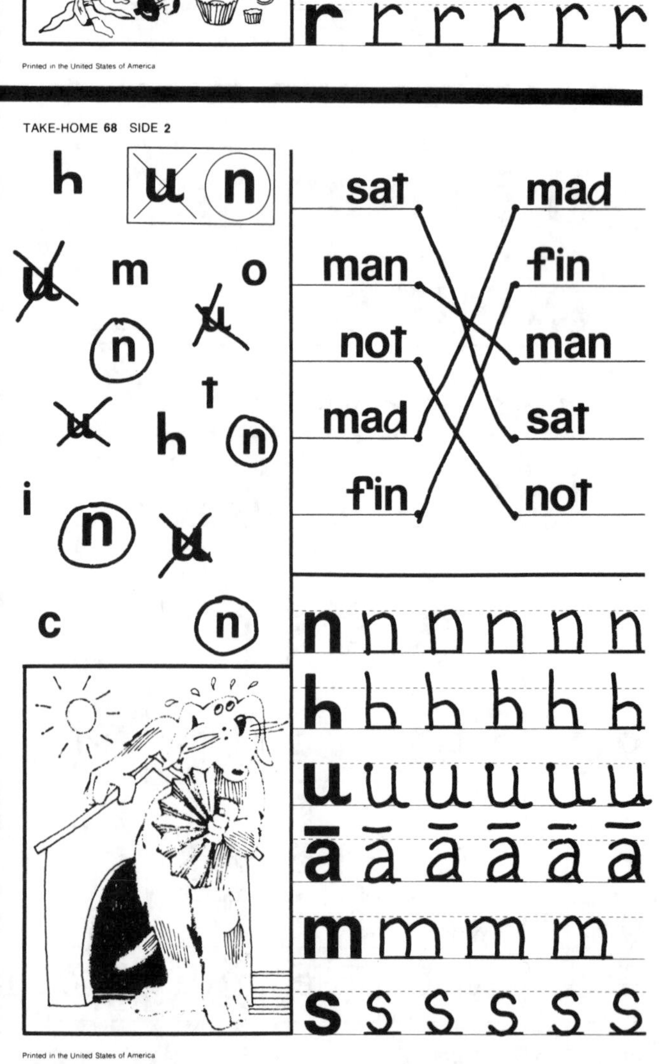
TAKE-HOME 68 SIDE 2
sat man not mad fin
mad fin man sat not
Printed in the United States of America

NAME ______ TAKE-HOME 69 SIDE 1 | TAKE-HOME 69 SIDE 2

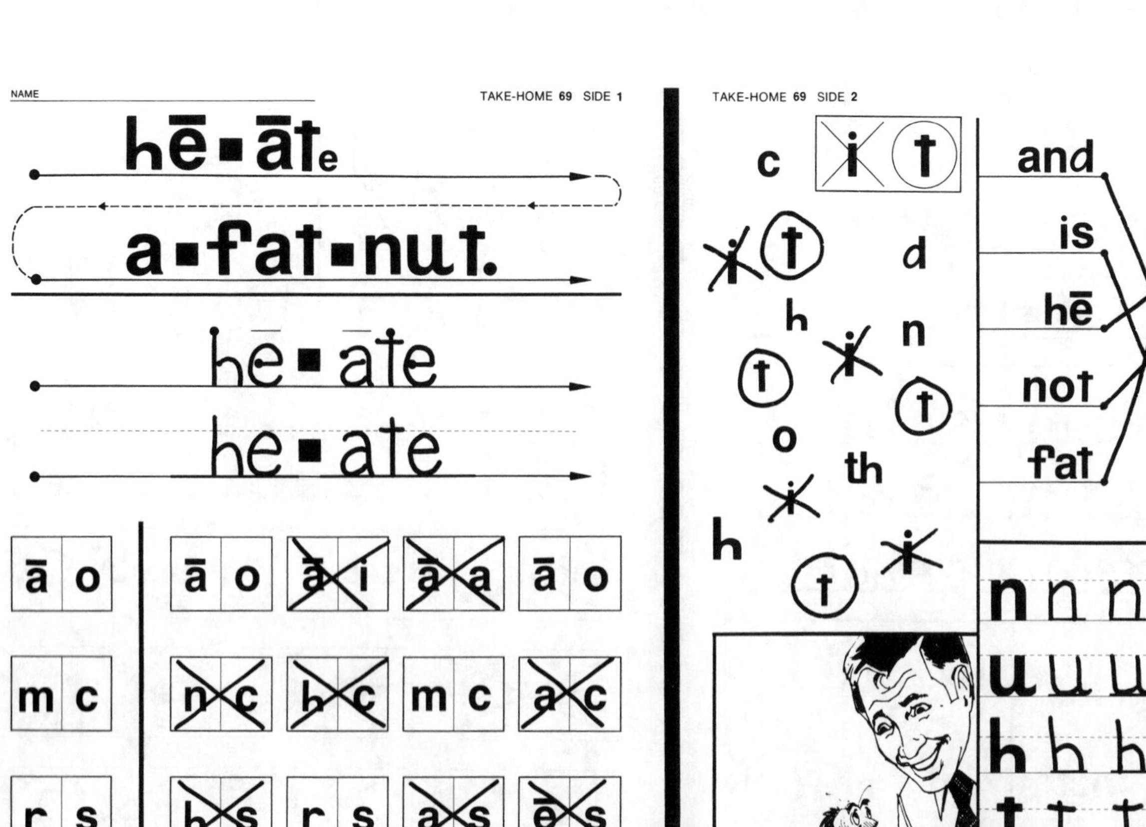

Printed in the United States of America

35

NAME ______ TAKE-HOME 70 SIDE 1 | TAKE-HOME 70 SIDE 2

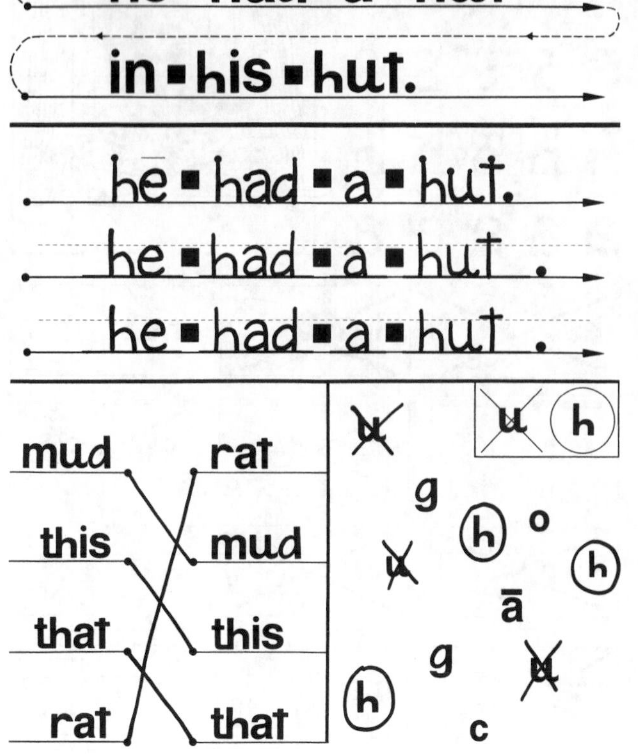

g u n h ā

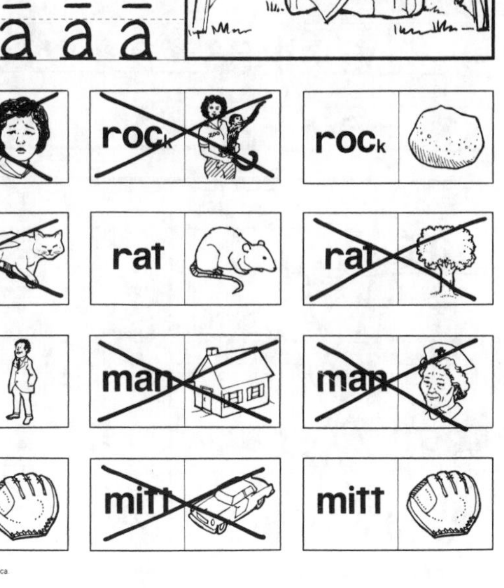

Printed in the United States of America

NAME ____________ TAKE-HOME 71 SIDE 1

thē ▪ sun ▪ is ▪ hot.
a ▪ man ▪ ran ▪ a
fan ▪ at ▪ us.

thē ▪ sun ▪ is ▪ hot.
the ▪ sun ▪ is ▪ hot.
the ▪ sun ▪ is ▪ hot.

mād$_e$	sic$_k$
āt$_e$	mad
mad	mād$_e$
sic$_k$	āt$_e$

t i
i o t c t h n t i i th

TAKE-HOME 71 SIDE 2

g g g g g
o o o o o
ā ā ā ā ā
c c c c c
t t t t t

sac$_k$ 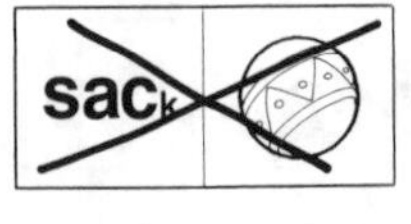 sac$_k$  sac$_k$ 

sit  sit  sit 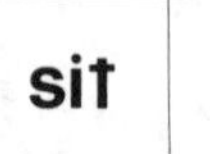

sad sad  sad 

hē  hē  hē 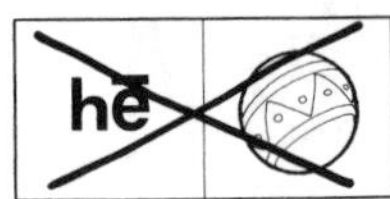

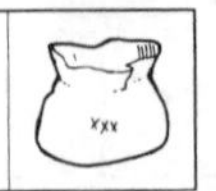

NAME ____________ TAKE-HOME 72 SIDE 1

hē ▪ has ▪ a ▪ rug.
that ▪ rug ▪ is
in ▪ his ▪ hut.

hē ▪ has ▪ a ▪ rug.
he ▪ has ▪ a ▪ rug.
he ▪ has ▪ a ▪ rug.

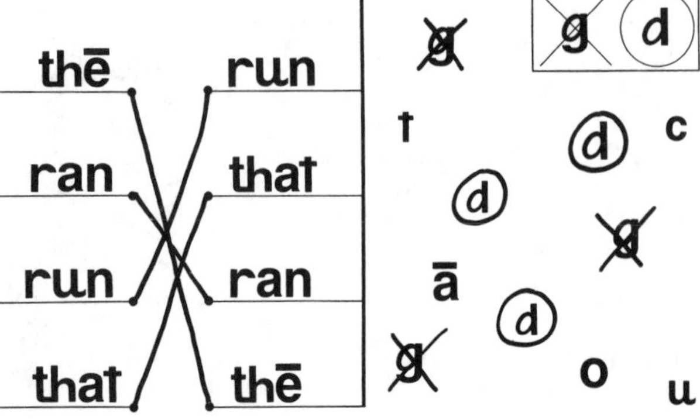

thē	run
ran	that
run	ran
that	thē

g d
g t d c d g ā d g o u

TAKE-HOME 72 SIDE 2

g g g g g
m m m m
s s s s s
h h h h h
a a a a a

nut  nut  nut 

fat 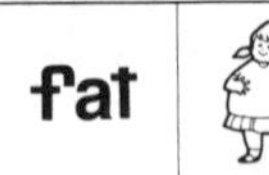 fat  fat  

sun  sun  sun 

mad  mad  mad 

NAME

TAKE-HOME 73 SIDE 1

hē is an ant.
hē has a sock
on his fēēt.

hē is an ant.
hē is an ant.
hē is an ant.

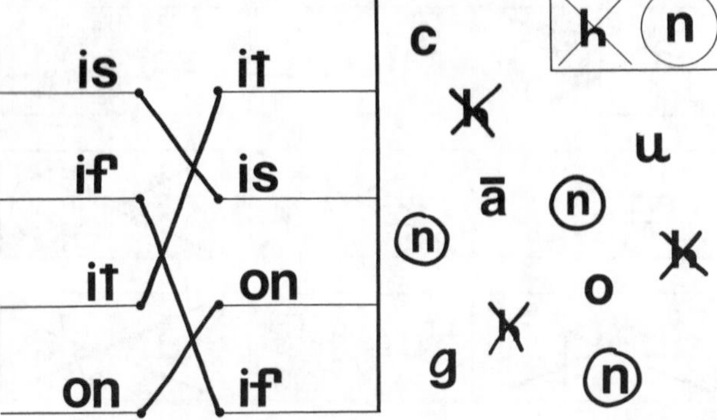

TAKE-HOME 73 SIDE 2

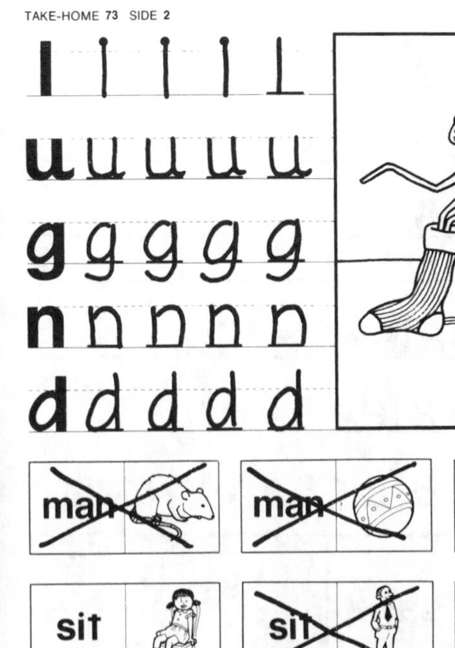

Printed in the United States of America

37

NAME

TAKE-HOME 74 SIDE 1

hē has an ant.
that ant āte
a fat sēēd.

hē has an ant.
he has an ant.
he has an ant.

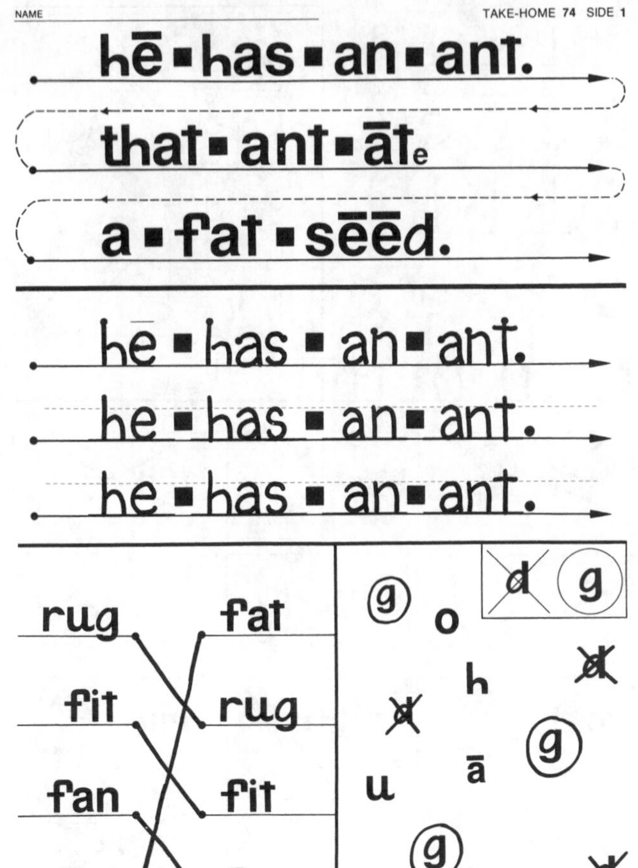

TAKE-HOME 74 SIDE 2

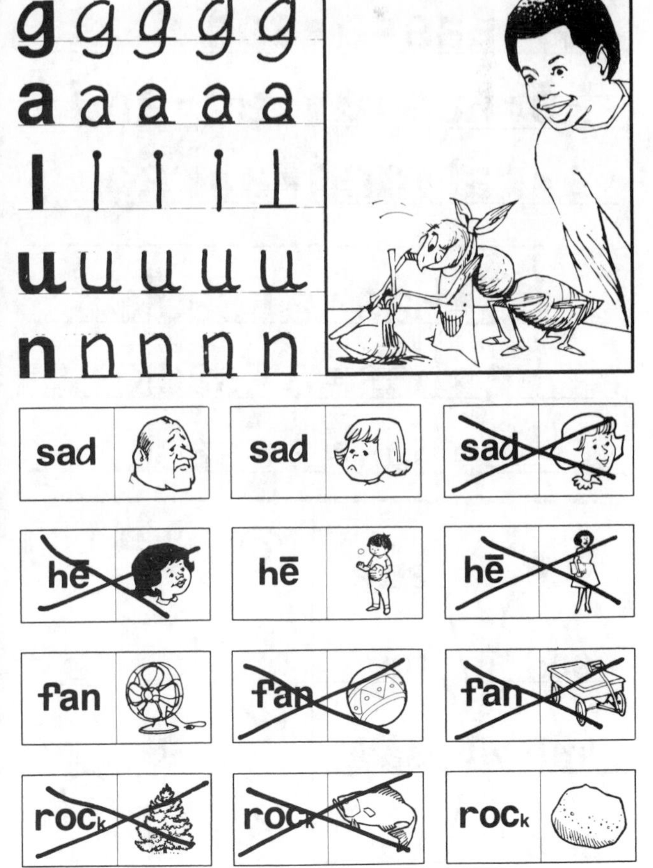

Printed in the United States of America

NAME ______________________ TAKE-HOME 75 SIDE 1

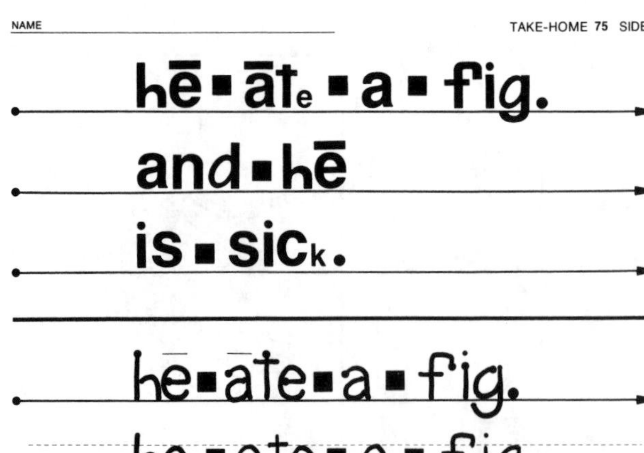

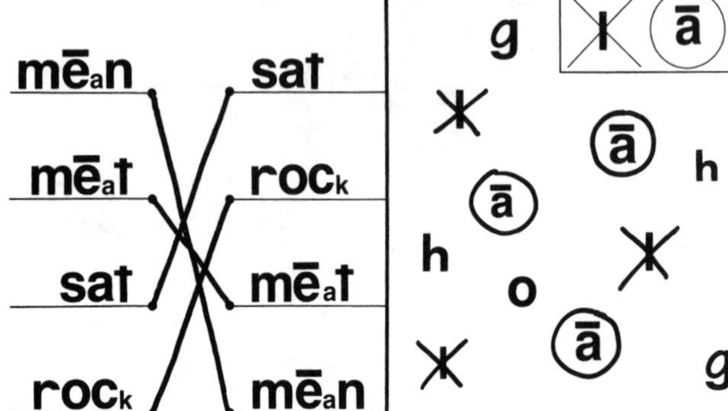

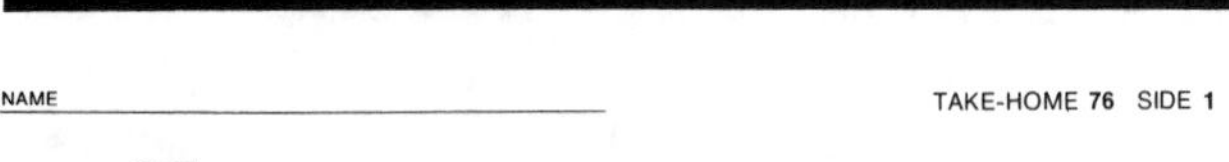

mēan sat
mēat rock
sat mēat
rock mēan

g ā h ā h o ā g

TAKE-HOME 75 SIDE 2

Printed in the United States of America

NAME ______________________ TAKE-HOME 76 SIDE 1

hē ▪ has ▪ a ▪ sack.
hē ▪ has ▪ a ▪ fan ▪ and
a ▪ rat ▪ and ▪ a ▪ rag.

hē ▪ has ▪ a ▪ sack.
he ▪ has ▪ a ▪ sack .
he ▪ has ▪ a ▪ sack .

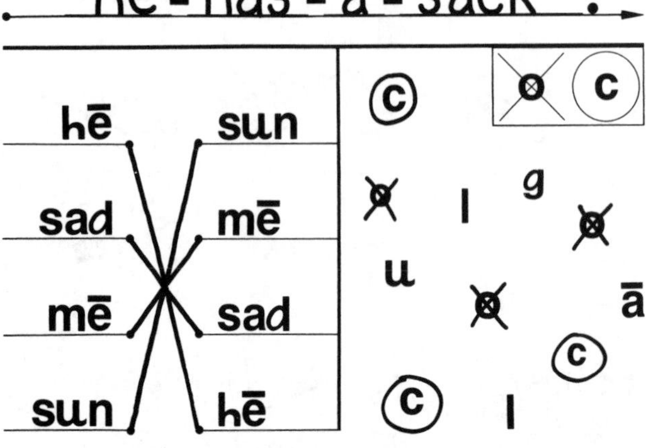

TAKE-HOME 76 SIDE 2

i i i i i
ē ē ē ē ē
l l l l l
o o o o o
m m m m m

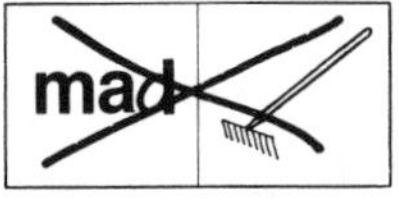

mad mad

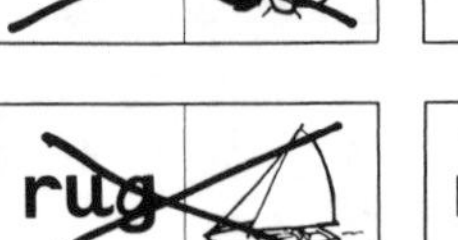

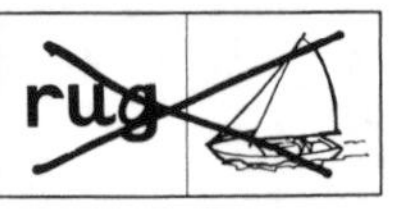

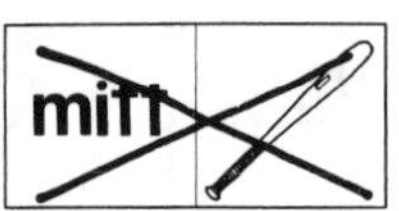

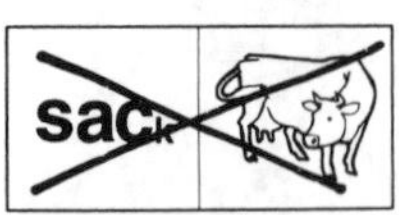

Printed in the United States of America

NAME ______________________ TAKE-HOME 77 SIDE 1

hē ▪ has ▪ fun.
hē ▪ is ▪ in ▪ thē ▪ rāin
and ▪ thē ▪ mud.

hē ▪ has ▪ fun.
he ▪ has ▪ fun.
he ▪ has ▪ fun.

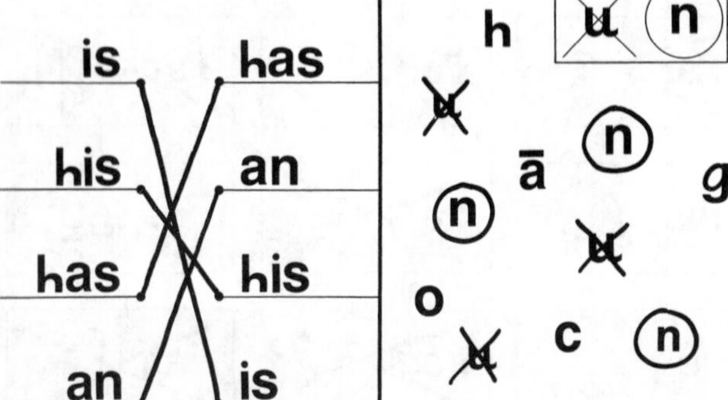

TAKE-HOME 77 SIDE 2

I I I I I
o o o o o
i i i i i
d d d d d
r r r r r

fan 
fan 
fan 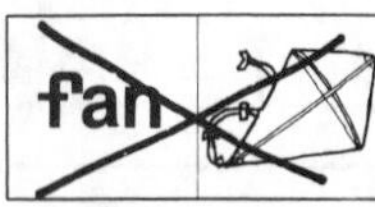

sad 
sad 
sad 

sit 
sit 
sit 

rag 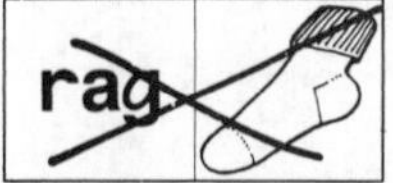
rag 
rag 

Printed in the United States of America

NAME ______________________ TAKE-HOME 78 SIDE 1

that ▪ man ▪ has ▪ thē ▪ māil.
hē ▪ is ▪ lāte.

hē ▪ has ▪ thē ▪ mail.
he ▪ has ▪ the ▪ mail .
he ▪ has ▪ the ▪ mail .

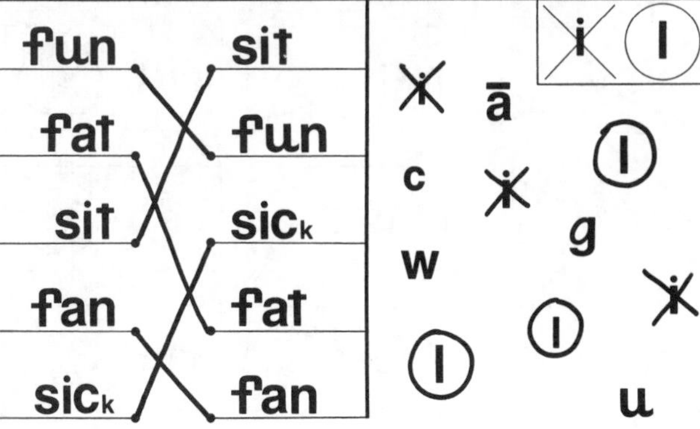

TAKE-HOME 78 SIDE 2

w w w w
n n n n n
l l l l l
t t t t t
a a a a a

mēan 
mēan 
mēan 

fat 
fat 
fat 

sick 
sick 
sick 
sick 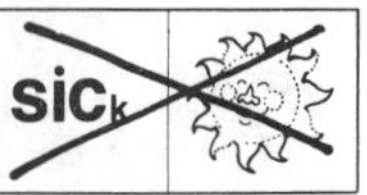

rock 
rock 
rock 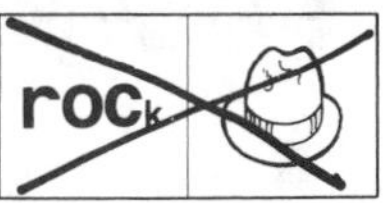

Printed in the United States of America

NAME ____________________

TAKE-HOME **79** SIDE **1**

thē ▪ lock ▪ is ▪ on ▪ a ▪ rock.

thē ▪ nut ▪ is ▪ on ▪ thē ▪ lock.

it ▪ is ▪ on ▪ a ▪ rock.

it ▪ is ▪ on ▪ a ▪ rock .

it ▪ is ▪ on ▪ a ▪ rock .

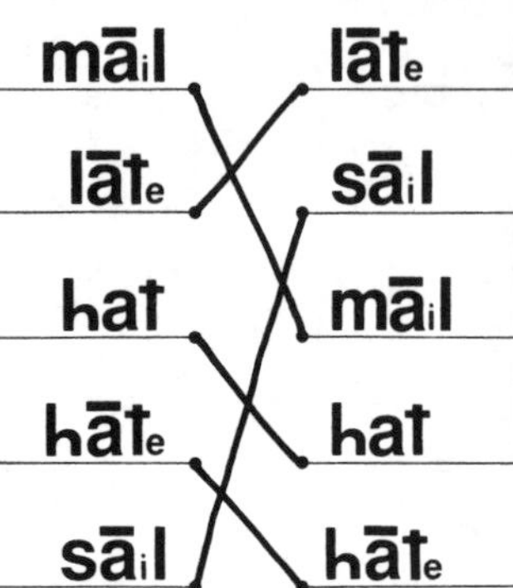

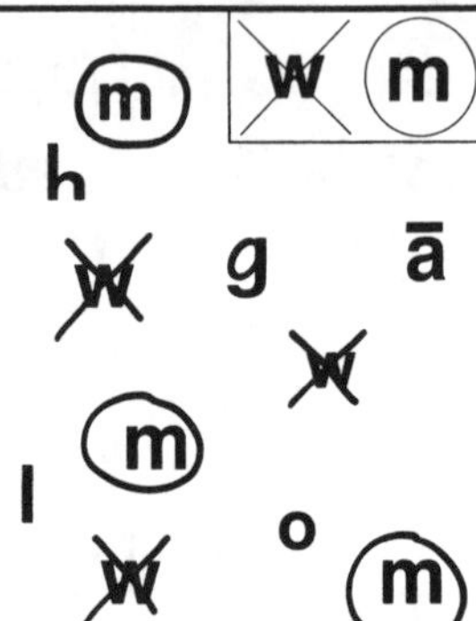

w m

m h w g ā w m l o w m

TAKE-HOME **79** SIDE **2**

l l l l l

w w w w

g g g g g

h h h h h

ā ā ā ā ā

sack 	sack 	sack 
fan 	fan 	fan 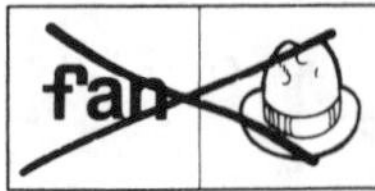
rat 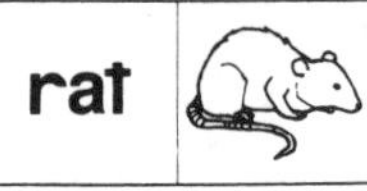	rat 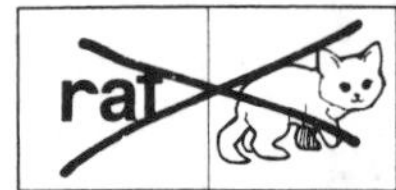	rat 
rag 	rag 	rag 

Printed in the United States of America

NAME ____________________

TAKE-HOME **80** SIDE **1**

wē ▪ sēē ▪ a ▪ hut. ▪ wē ▪ will

run ▪ in ▪ thē ▪ hut.

wē ▪ will ▪ lock ▪ thē ▪ hut.

wē ▪ sēē ▪ a ▪ hut.

we ▪ see ▪ a ▪ hut .

we ▪ see ▪ a ▪ hut .

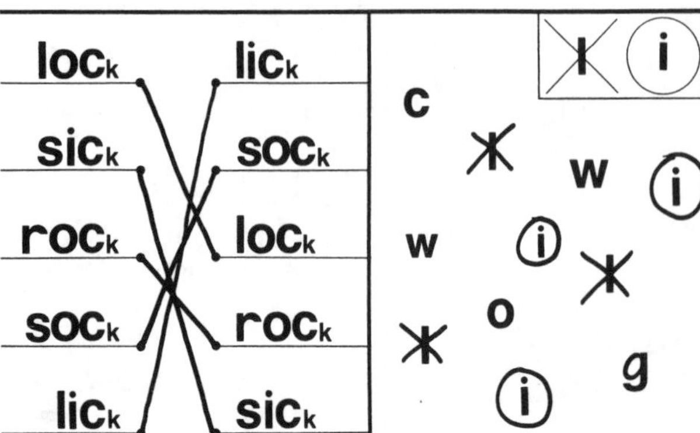

TAKE-HOME **80** SIDE **2**

w w w w

g g g g g

c c c c c

l l l l l

o o o o o

hē 	hē 	hē 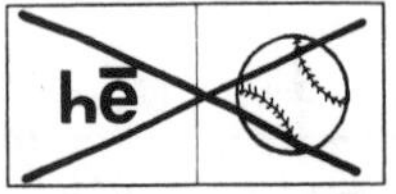
nut 	nut 	nut 
rāin 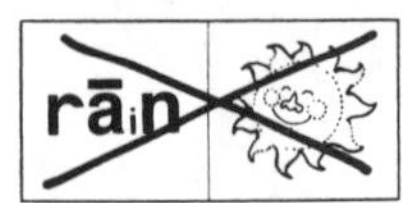	rāin 	rāin 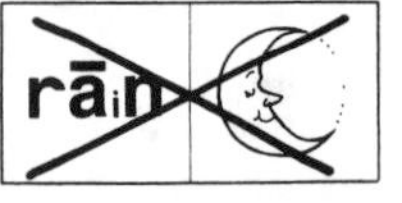
fun 	fun 	fun 

Printed in the United States of America

NAME ______________________

his ▪ nāmₑ ▪ is ▪ ron.

hē ▪ will ▪ run. ▪ and

hē ▪ will ▪ sēē ▪ mē.

his ▪ name ▪ is ▪ ron.

his ▪ name ▪ is ▪ ron .

his ▪ name ▪ is ▪ ron .

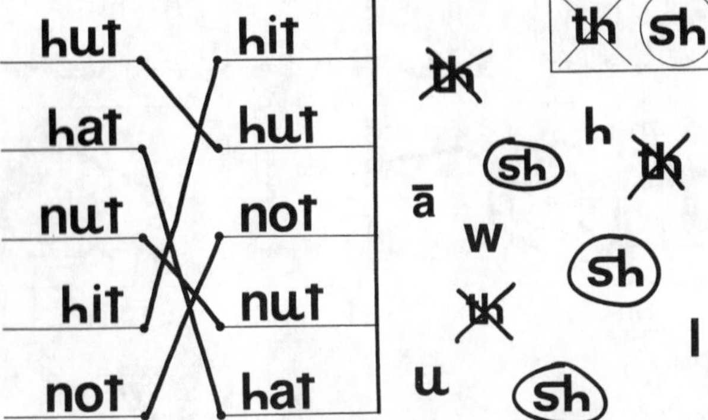

hut	hit
hat	hut
nut	not
hit	nut
not	hat

th sh

th h th sh ā w sh th l u sh

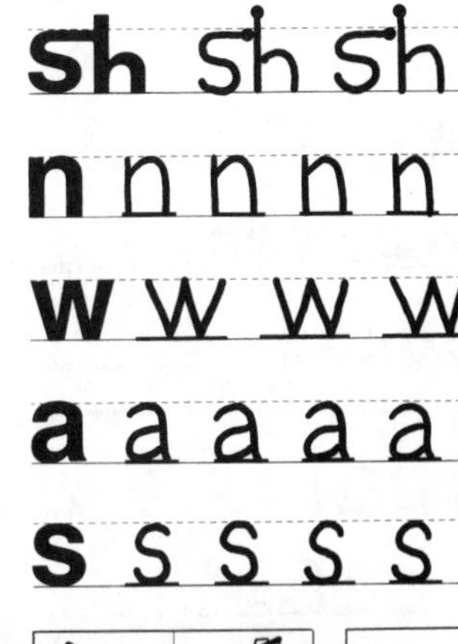

sh sh sh

n n n n n

w w w w

a a a a a

s s s s s

rug 	rug 	rug 
sit  	sit 	sit 
sacₖ 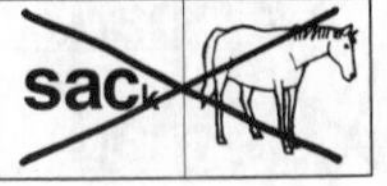	sacₖ 	sacₖ 
māᵢl 	māᵢl  	māᵢl 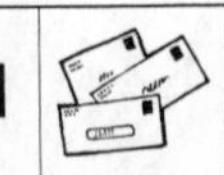

Printed in the United States of America

NAME ______________________

wē · had · a · ram.

that · ram · ran.

wē · ran · and

hē · ran.

wē · had · a · ram.

we · had · a · ram .

we · had · a · ram .

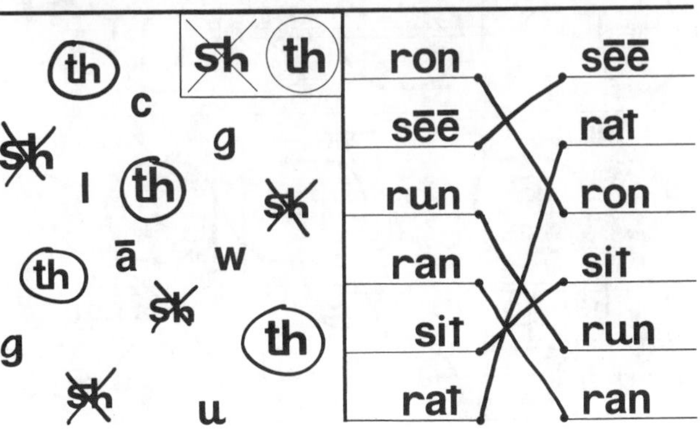

sh th

th c g sh l th sh th ā w sh th g sh u

ron	sēē
sēē	rat
run	ron
ran	sit
sit	run
rat	ran

sh sh sh

w w w w

g g g g g

u u u u u

a nut 	a man 	rocₖ 
sad 	rat 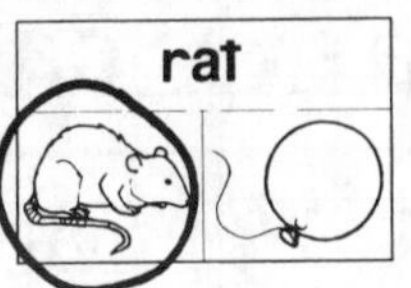	a sacₖ 
rag 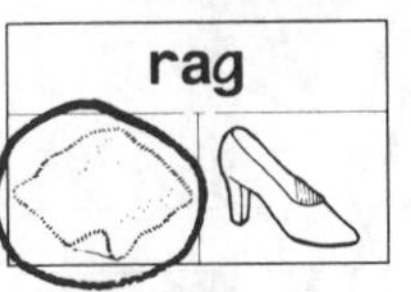	a locₖ 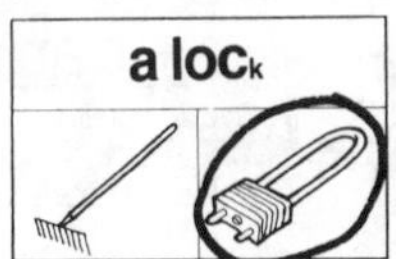	run 
a rug 	sit 	a hat 

Printed in the United States of America

NAME 

TAKE-HOME **83** SIDE **1**

this · is · a · cat.

this · cat · has · fat

fēēt. · this · cat · can

run · in · thē · mud.

this · is · a · cat.

this · is · a · cat.

this · is · a · cat.

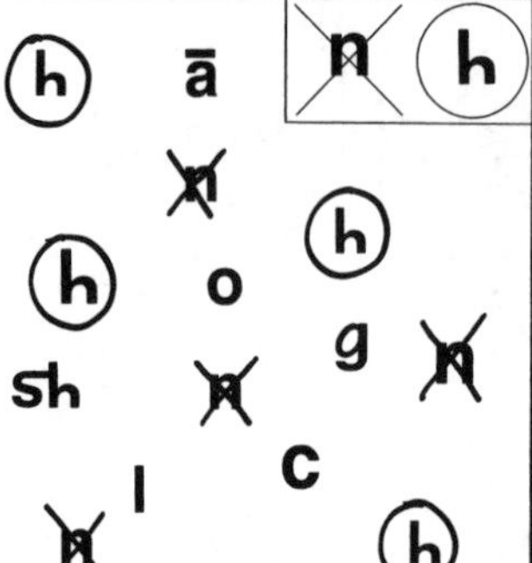

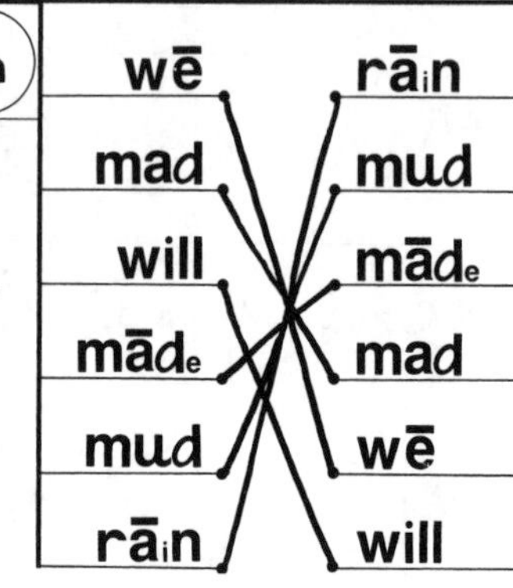

TAKE-HOME **83** SIDE **2**

th th th th

sh sh sh

w w w w

g g g g g

hut	a lock	a fan
		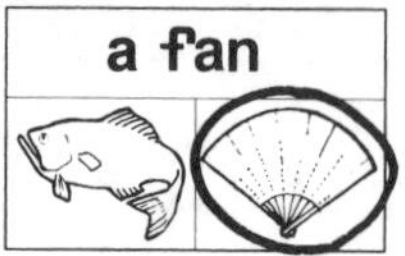
hē	**run**	**māil**

mad	**rāin**	**a rock**

sick	**fat**	**mitt**

Printed in the United States of America

NAME

TAKE-HOME **84** SIDE **1**

shē · has · a · cat.

that · cat · is

not · little. · that · cat

is · fat.

shē · has · a · cat.

she · has · a · cat.

she · has · a · cat.

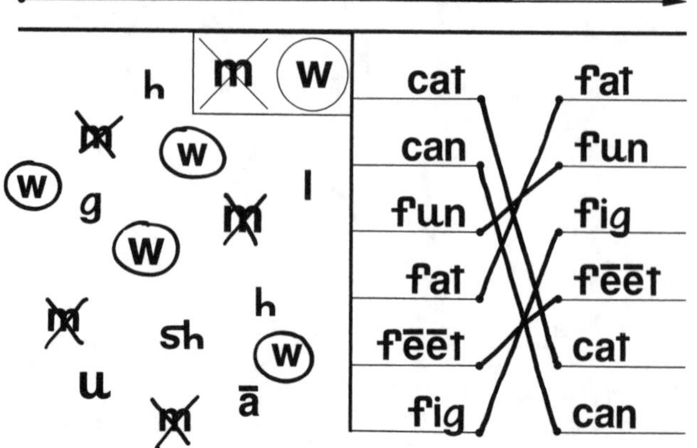

TAKE-HOME **84** SIDE **2**

th th th th

a a a a a

sh sh sh

l l l l l

a sack	sit	nut
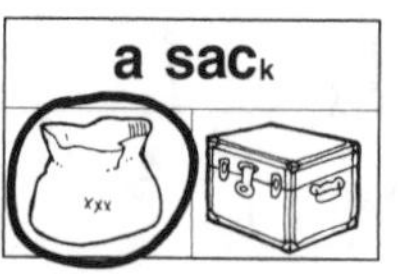	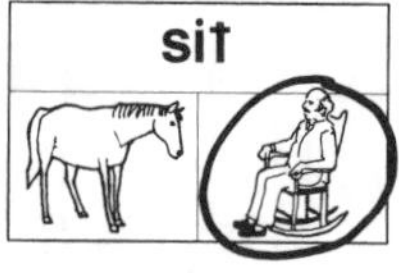	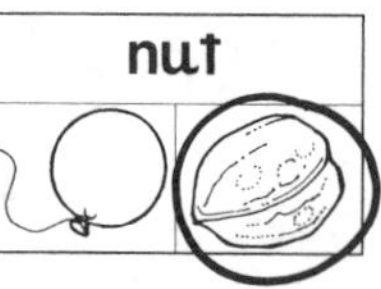
man	**a rag**	**mēan**

mud	**rain**	**mail**
		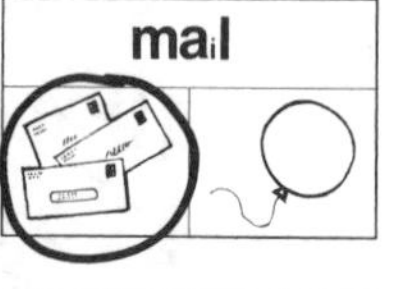
hē	**rug**	**a hut**

Printed in the United States of America

NAME _______________ TAKE-HOME **85** SIDE 1

hē·has·a·shack.
thē·shack·is·in·thē
sand.·thē·man·is
in·thē·shack.

hē · has · a · shack.
he · has · a · shack .
he · has · a · shack .

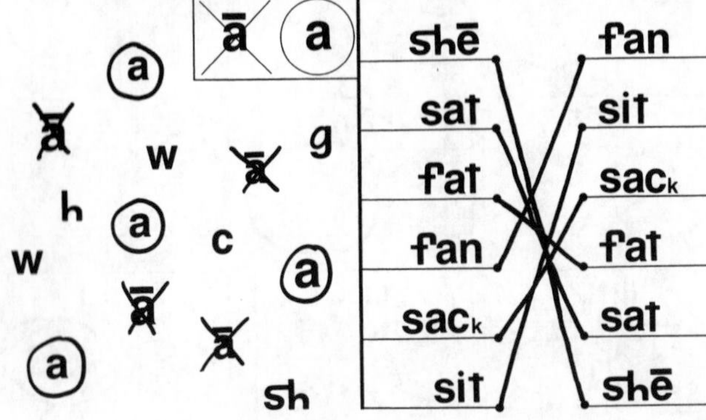

TAKE-HOME **85** SIDE 2

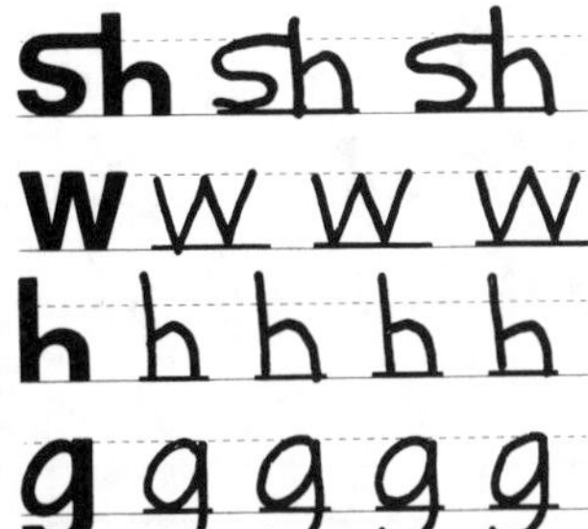

lock
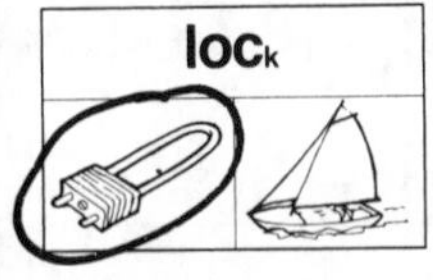

run

mad

a fan
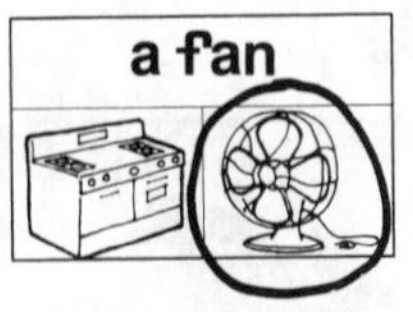

mitt

rāin

sick

sad

a rock

fat

hē

mēan

Printed in the United States of America

NAME _______________ TAKE-HOME **86** SIDE 1

hē·had·fun.
shē·had·fun·in·thē
sand.·and·thē·cat·had
fun·in·thē·sand.

hē · had · fun.
he · had · fun.
he · had · fun.

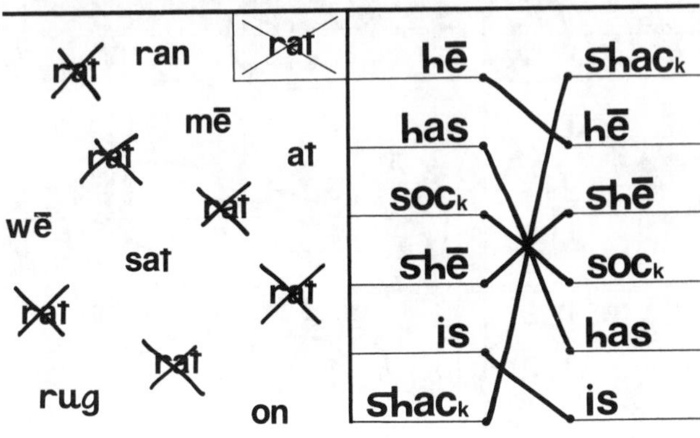

TAKE-HOME **86** SIDE 2

o o o o o
a a a a a
ā ā ā ā ā
u u u u u

a rat
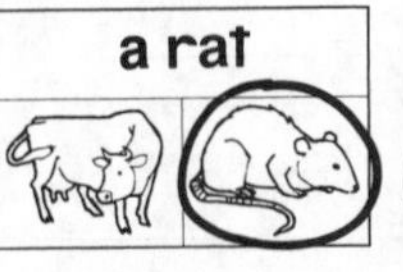

hut

man

him

sad

a rock

sit

a sack

run

fēēt
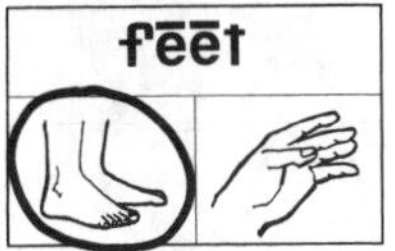

cat

mail

Printed in the United States of America

NAME ______________________ TAKE-HOME **87** SIDE **1**

shē is in thē rāin.
shē has a sack. māil is
in that sack. will shē rēad
thē māil?

shē is in the rain.
she is in the rain.
she is in the rain.

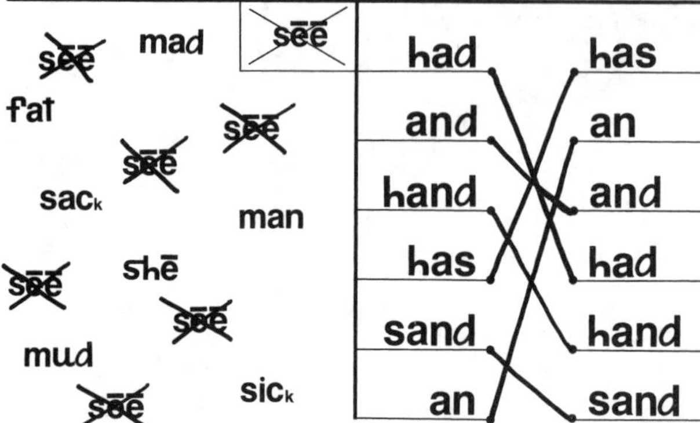

see mad see
fat see see
sack man
see shē
see mud
see sick

had	has
and	an
hand	and
has	had
sand	hand
an	sand

TAKE-HOME **87** SIDE **2**

i i i i i
u u u u u
w w w w
g g g g g

a cat	fat	lock
hē	run	a mitt
fēēt	rāin	shē
little	sick	a rug

Printed in the United States of America

NAME ______________________ TAKE-HOME **88** SIDE **1**

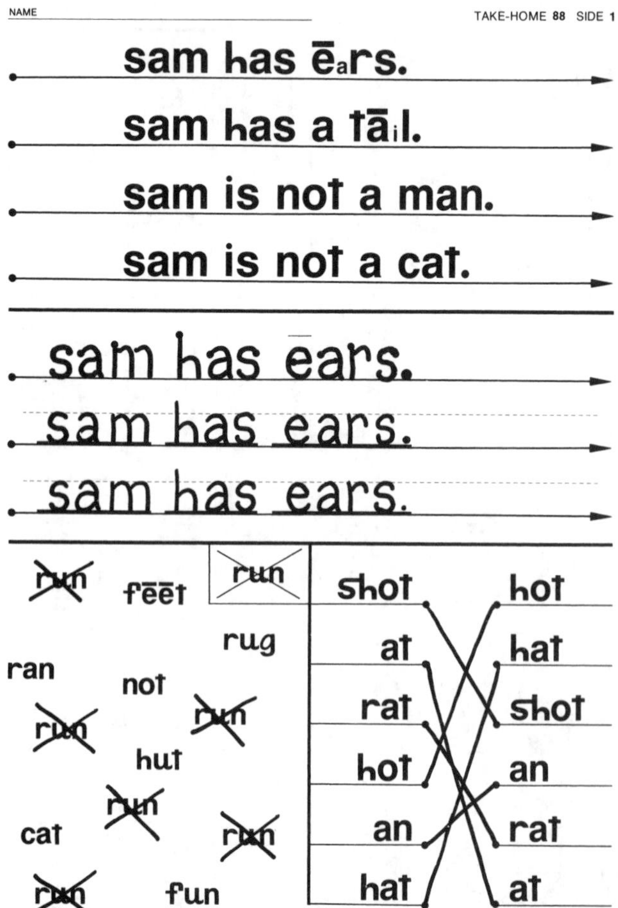

sam has ēars.
sam has a tāil.
sam is not a man.
sam is not a cat.

sam has ears.
sam has ears.
sam has ears.

run fēēt run
rug
ran not run
run hut
run
cat run
run fun

shot	hot
at	hat
rat	shot
hot	an
an	rat
hat	at

TAKE-HOME **88** SIDE **2**

sh sh sh
n n n n n
l l l l l
th th th th

shack	sand	sad
shē	mud	a rock
him	sit	cat
mēan	māil	a fan

Printed in the United States of America

NAME

thē sand is hot.
his fēēt got
hot. his hat is
not hot.

the sand is hot.
the sand is hot.
the sand is hot.

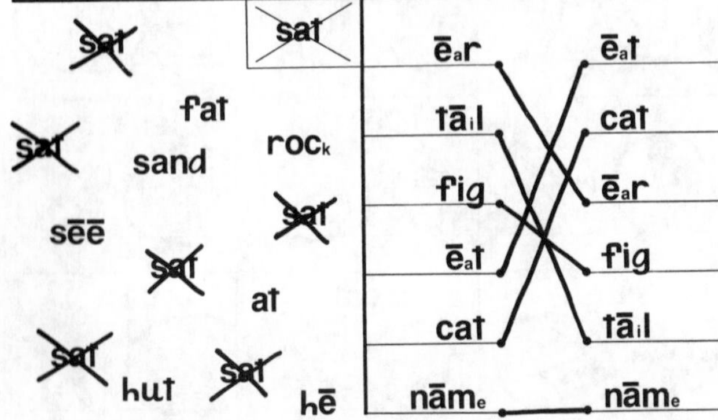

h h h h h
n n n n n
w w w w
r r r r r

sack

fēēt

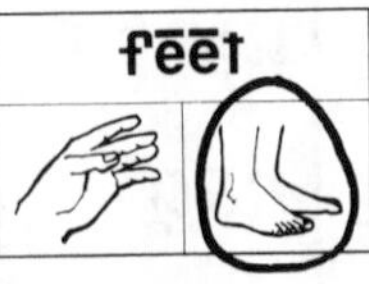

a lock

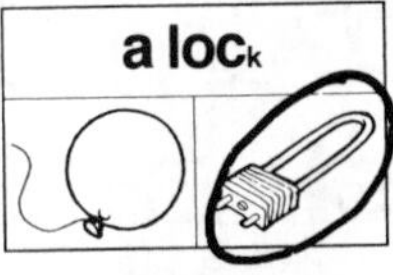

a rug

shē

fat

shack

rāin

hē

mad

little

fan

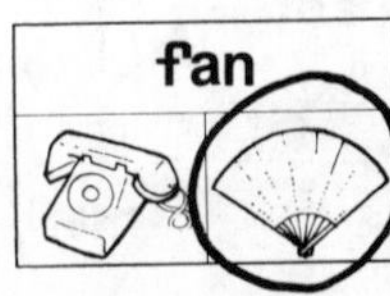

Printed in the United States of America

NAME

a fish māde a wish.
"I wish I had fēēt. I wish
I had a tāil. I wish I had
a hat. I wish I had a dish."

a fish made a wish.
a fish made a wish.
a fish made a wish.

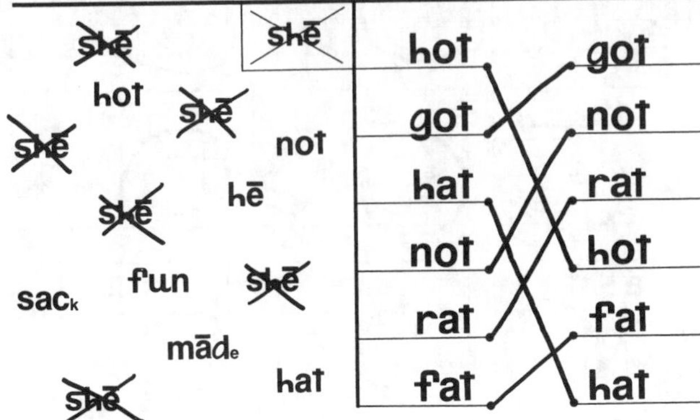

f f f f f
a a a a a
I I I I
r r r r r

rag

sand

a hut

a rat

run

shē

māil

a rug

rock

cat

sick

him

Printed in the United States of America

NAME ______________________ 

TAKE-HOME 91 SIDE 1

now I will run.

now I will run.

now I will run.

now I will run.

I I I I	hat	rag
sh sh sh	rag	hat
w w w w	hot	fat
l l l l l	fat	am
g g g g g	am	hot

~~sit~~

~~sit~~ hit it ~~sit~~ ~~sit~~ fēēt ~~sit~~ sat locₖ hut ~~sit~~ wish ~~sit~~ not ~~sit~~ ~~sit~~ ~~sit~~ mad ~~sit~~

TAKE-HOME 91 SIDE 2

A picture that shows "now I will run."

a nut

fat

shē

tāil
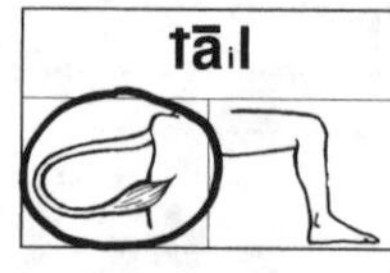

a man

ēars
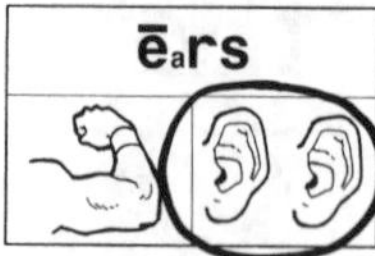

sit

fēēt
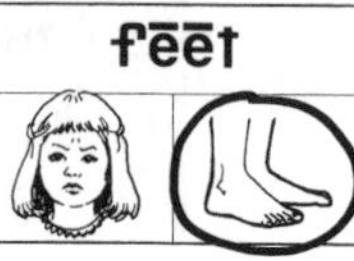

shacₖ

rug

a cat

rāin

Printed in the United States of America

NAME ______________________

TAKE-HOME 92 SIDE 1

I wish I had sand.

I wish I had sand.

I wish I had sand.

I wish I had sand.

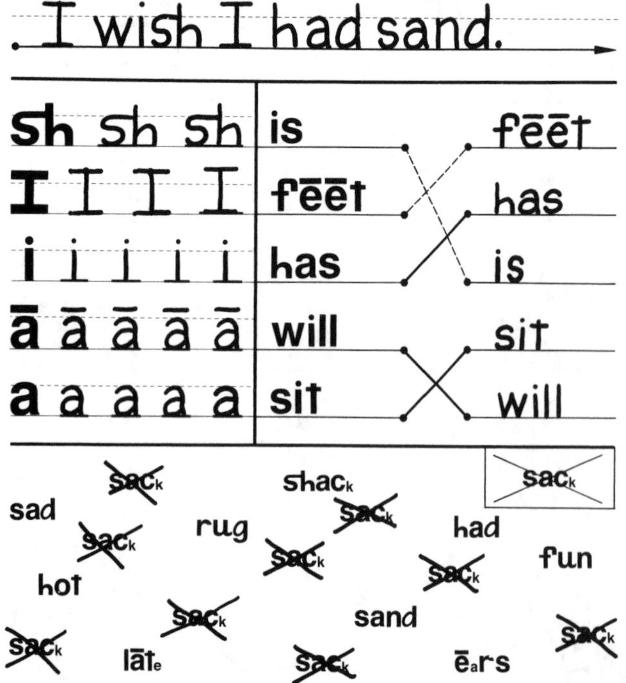

sh sh sh	is	fēēt
I I I I	fēēt	has
i i i i i	has	is
ā ā ā ā ā	will	sit
a a a a a	sit	will

~~sacₖ~~

~~sacₖ~~ sad shacₖ ~~sacₖ~~ ~~sacₖ~~ rug had ~~sacₖ~~ fun hot ~~sacₖ~~ ~~sacₖ~~ sand ~~sacₖ~~ ~~sacₖ~~ lāte ~~sacₖ~~ ēars

TAKE-HOME 92 SIDE 2

A picture that shows "I wish I had sand."

a tāil
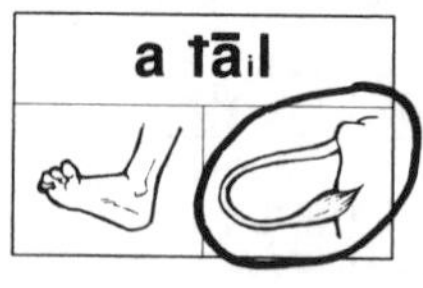

run

rocₖ

him

sacₖ
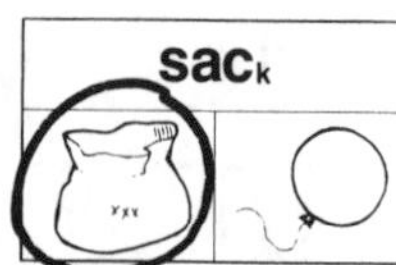

mad

māil

sand

fēēt
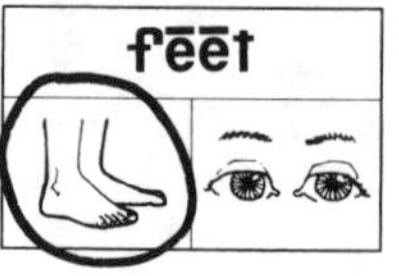

a hat

ēars
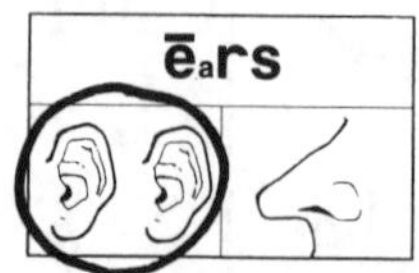

littlₑ
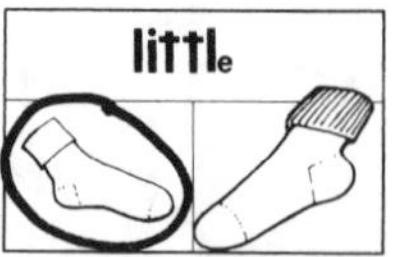

Printed in the United States of America

NAME ______ TAKE-HOME 93 SIDE 1

the cat has fun.

the cat has fun.

the cat has fun.

the cat has fun.

w w w w	fish	at
c c c c c	and	fish
o o o o o	at	and
sh sh sh	nāme	hē
ā ā ā ā ā	hē	nāme

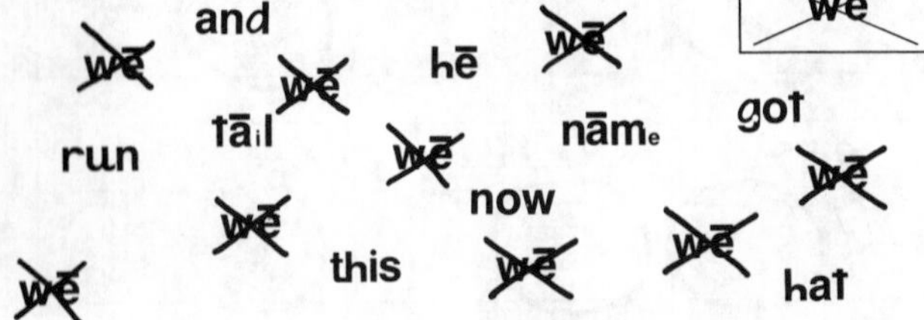

wē

and wē wē hē wē run tāil wē nāme got now wē wē this wē wē hat wē

TAKE-HOME 93 SIDE 2

A picture that shows "the cat has fun."

hat

a rat
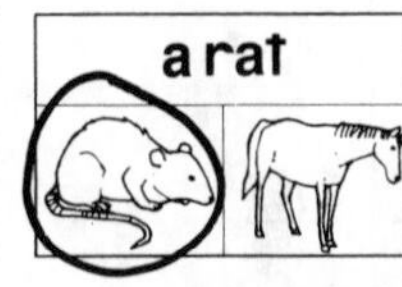

shē

a fish
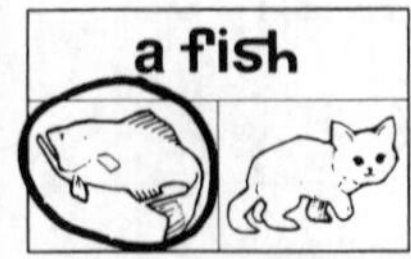

rāin

sad

a mitt

dish

ēars
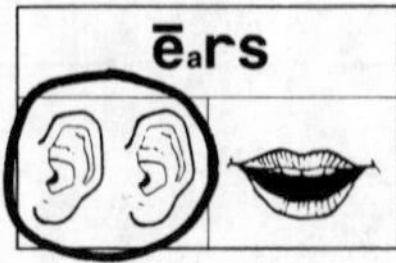

a cat

fan
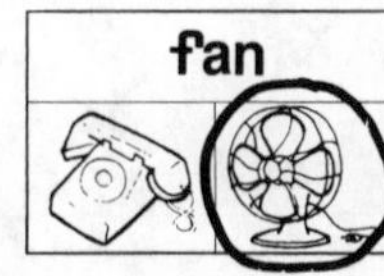

hē

NAME ______ TAKE-HOME 94 SIDE 1

the fish had fun.

the fish had fun.

the fish had fun.

the fish had fun.

k k k k k	had	mom
c c c c c	mom	ham
o o o o o	fun	had
d d d d d	ham	fun
t t t t t	shē	shē

this

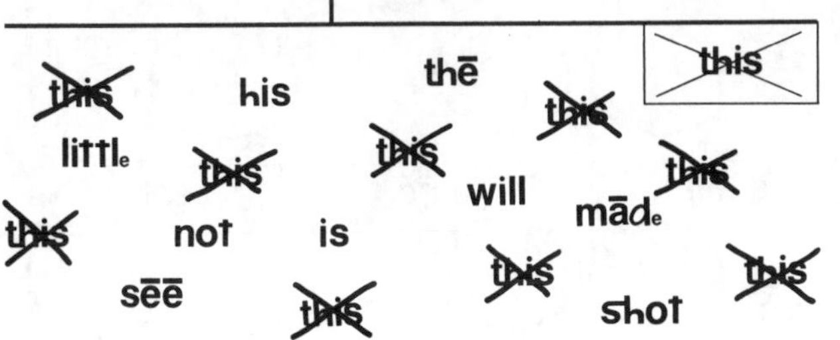

this his thē this littl this this will this this not is mād this sēē this this shot

TAKE-HOME 94 SIDE 2

a picture that shows "the fish had fun."

a fish

fat

sit
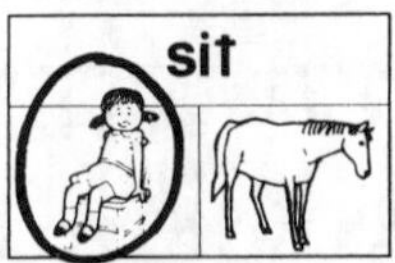

hill

fēēt
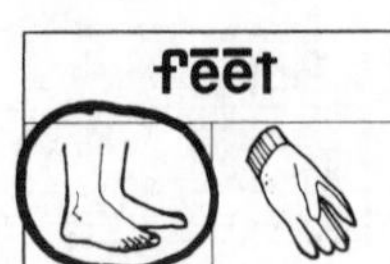

a rug

a man

sand

hut

hat
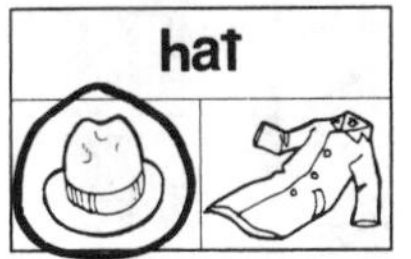

a dish

tāil
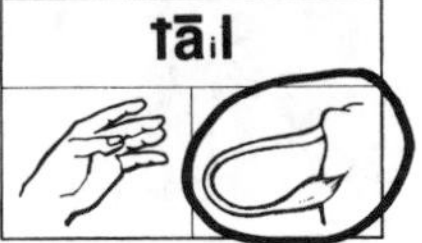

NAME

shē sat on a hill.

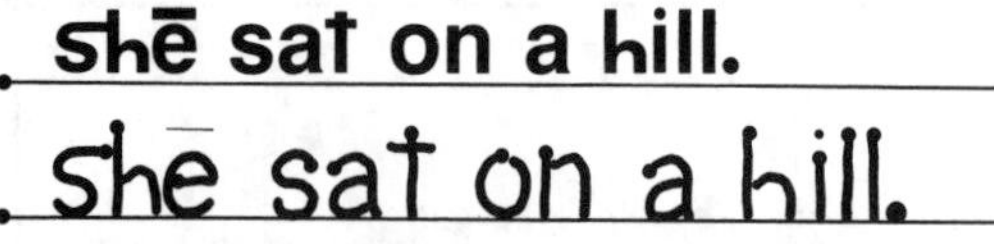

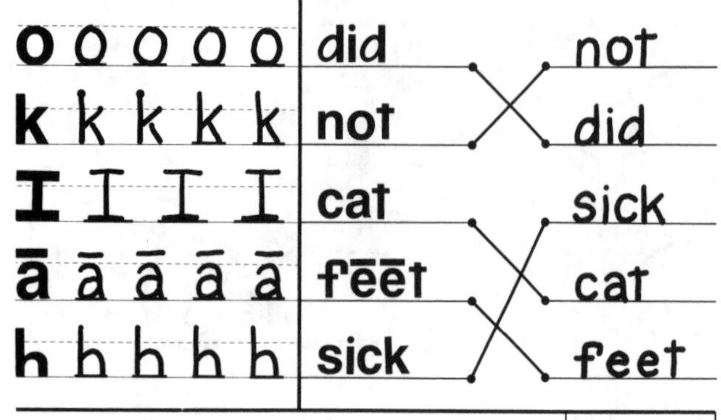

A picture that shows "she sat on a hill."

a dish	shē	rag

fēēt	**shack**	**a mitt**
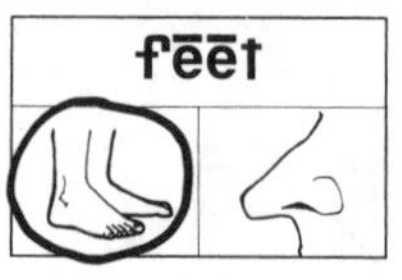		
a rāke	**him**	**fan**

ēars	**lāke**	**sit**
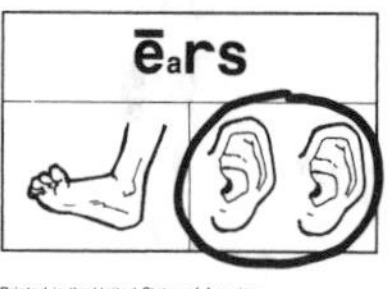		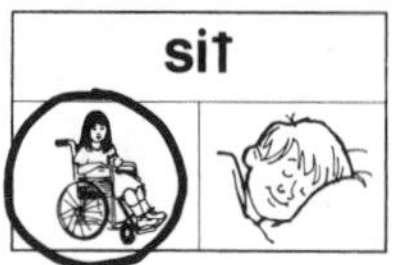

NAME

shē said, "I āte."

she said, "I ate."

she said, "I ate."

she said, "I ate."

n n n n n
k k k k k
c c c c c
m m m m
th th th

is
his
sēē
hat
sand

hat
his
is
sand
see

shē

shē said fēēt
shack shē shē
hē shē
shē little shē
got shē
shē cow shē shē thē tāil

A picture that shows "she said 'I ate.'"

rāke	a dish	cat

mom	**tāil**	**little**
	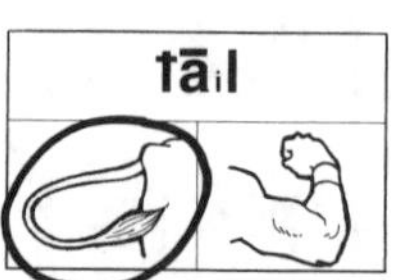	
sand	**a rag**	**lāke**

a hill	**ēars**	**sack**
	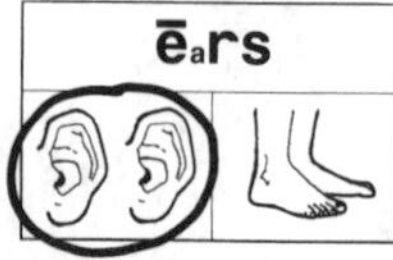	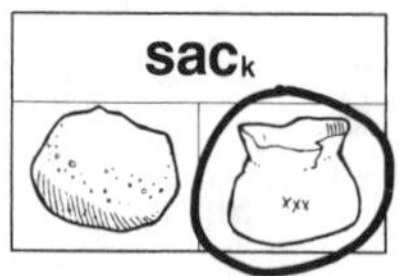

NAME

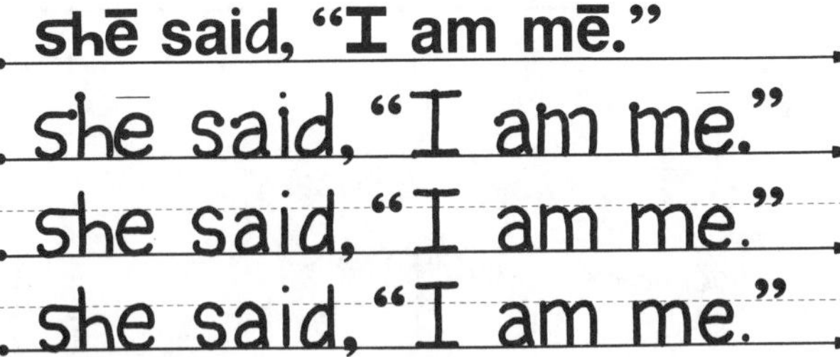

h h h h h	rock	fat
d d d d d	māil	rock
k k k k k	fat	mail
s s s s s	fun	we
ē ē ē ē ē	wē	fun

that

that fish that āte hot that at that that fat that mom now this gun that that that

A picture that shows "she said 'I am me.'"

hill 	hē 	sad 
a lock 	fat 	hut 
a fish 	mom 	fēēt 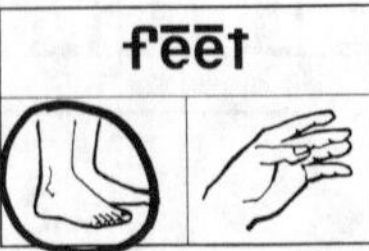
tāil 	rāin 	a fan 

NAME

shē was not mad.
she was not mad.
she was not mad.
she was not mad.

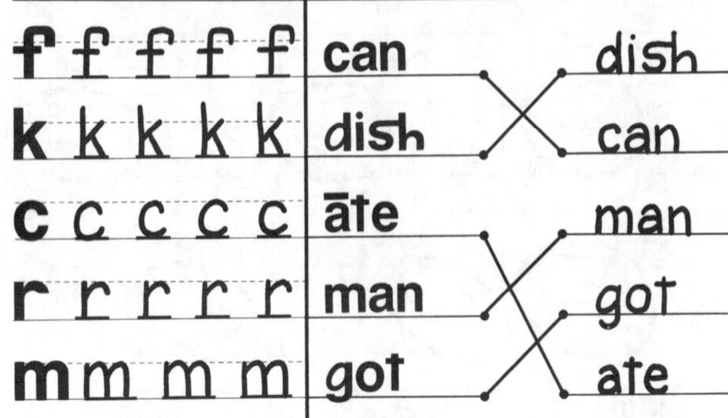

nō

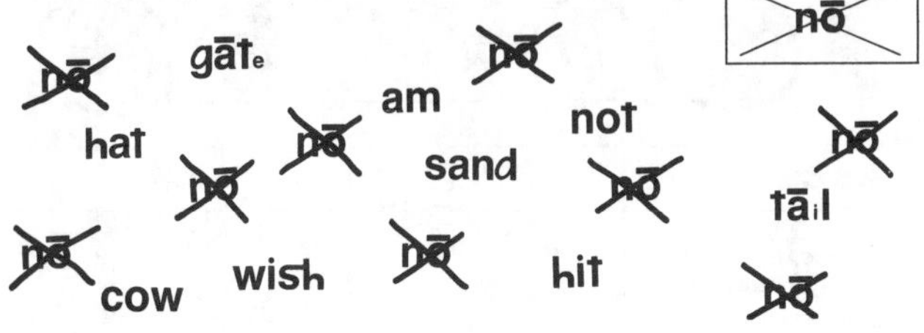

A picture that shows "she was not mad."

gāte 	a cow 	māil 
dish 	sock 	a cat 
shē 	a rāke 	rāin 
him 	a shack 	hill 

NAME ______________________

TAKE-HOME **99** SIDE **1**

hē sat with a cat.

hē sat with a cat.

he sat with a cat.

he sat with a cat.

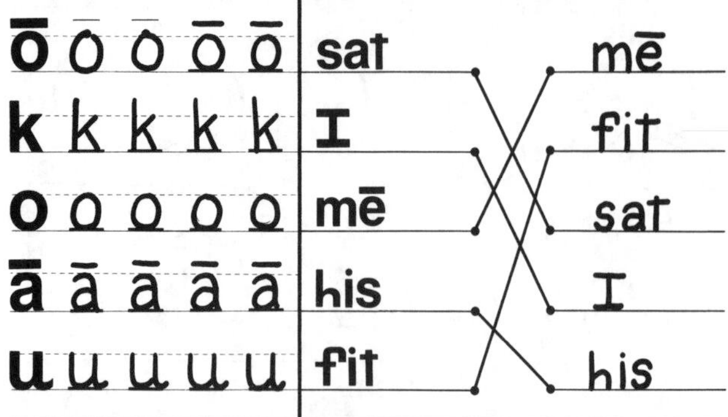

ō ō ō ō ō	sat	mē
k k k k k	I	fit
o o o o o	mē	sat
ā ā ā ā ā	his	I
u u u u u	fit	his

~~thē~~ shē cat ~~thē~~ ~~thē~~

hē ~~thē~~ āte ~~thē~~ fish hug ~~thē~~

~~thē~~ little ~~thē~~ ~~thē~~

nō ~~thē~~ lick

TAKE-HOME **99** SIDE **2**

A picture that shows "he sat with a cat."

a cow	fan	fish
	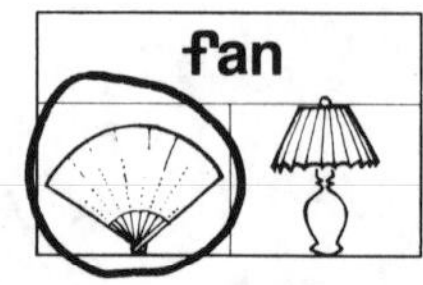	

lāke	mom	sand

ēars	a mitt	fēēt
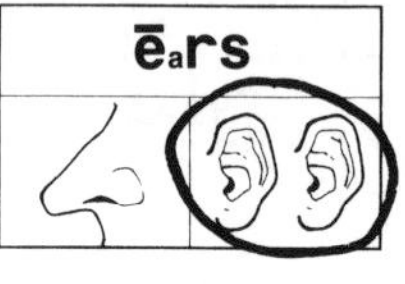		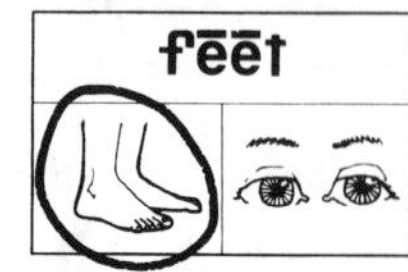

a rag	lock	him
	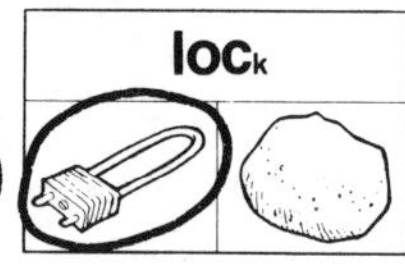	

Printed in the United States of America

NAME ______________________

TAKE-HOME **100** SIDE **1**

hē has nō tēēth.

hē has nō tēēth.

he has no teeth.

he has no teeth.

k k k k k	kick	said
o o o o o	got	kick
ō ō ō ō ō	said	with
m m m m	cow	got
ē ē ē ē ē	with	cow

~~if~~ him

~~if~~ said ~~if~~

nō kick ~~if~~

now ~~if~~ ~~if~~ ~~if~~

thē rug ~~if~~

~~if~~ wish ~~if~~ fēēl

TAKE-HOME **100** SIDE **2**

A picture that shows "he has no teeth."

lāke	cow	tāil
		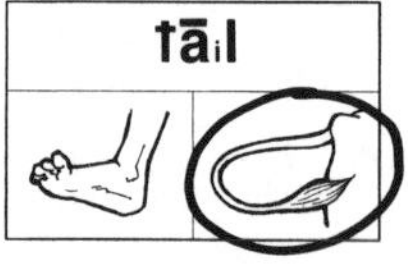

shē	dish	a rāke

hill	a shack	sick

a cat	sack	fat
	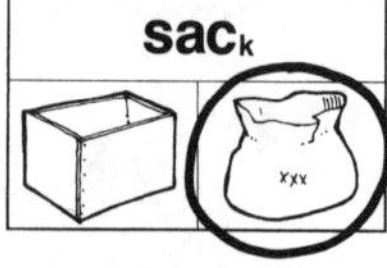	

Printed in the United States of America

NAME ____________________ TAKE-HOME 101 SIDE 1

I can kiss a cat.

I can kiss a cat.

I can kiss a cat.

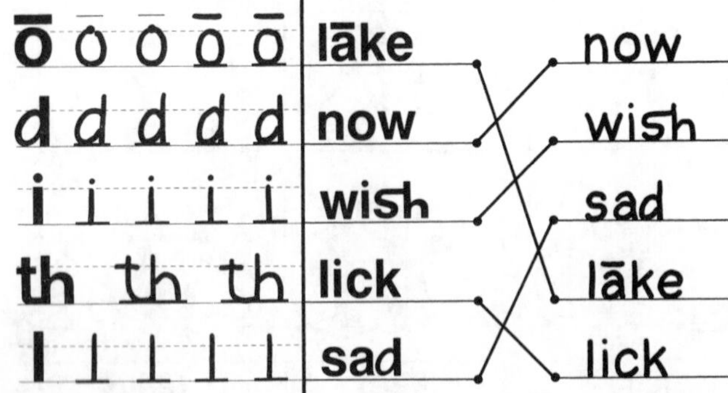

him

hit him hat cāke hug nō ēat kiss if will

TAKE-HOME 101 SIDE 2

A picture that shows "I can kiss a cat."

a rug

fēēt

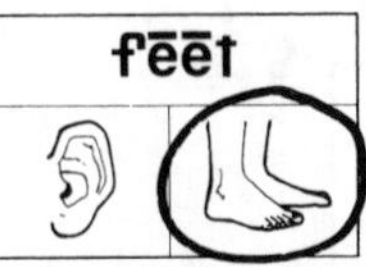

him

hut

māil

ēars

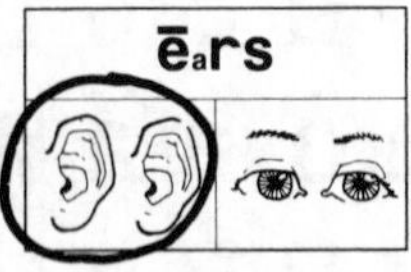

kiss

mom

a lāke

a rock

hat

lick

Printed in the United States of America

NAME ____________________ TAKE-HOME 102 SIDE 1

a cat is on thē cow.

a cat is on thē cow.

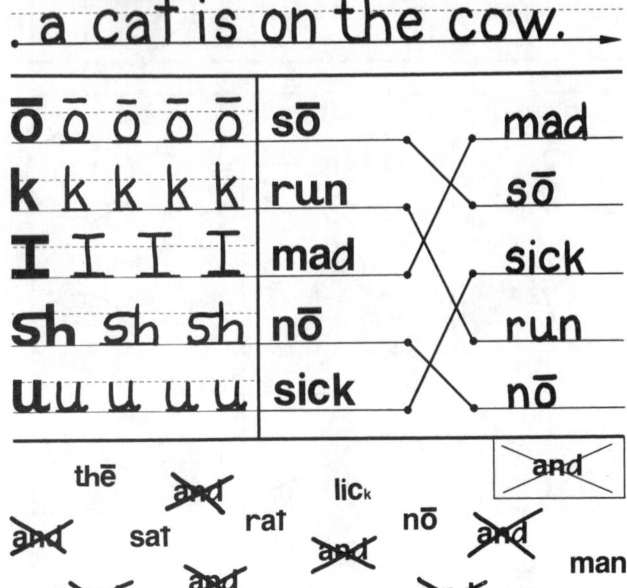

TAKE-HOME 102 SIDE 2

a picture that shows "a cat is on the cow."

a cat

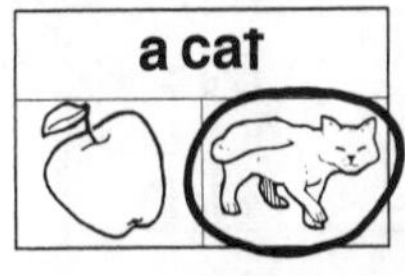

sand

shē

sad

a fish

shack

a rāke

sit

a cow

lock

hē

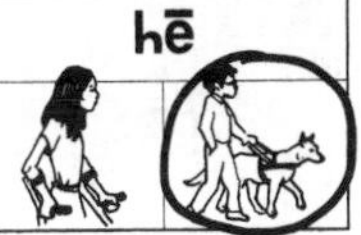

mitt

Printed in the United States of America

NAME ______________________

I can hōld thē hats.

I can hold the hats.

I can hold the hats.

I can hold the hats.

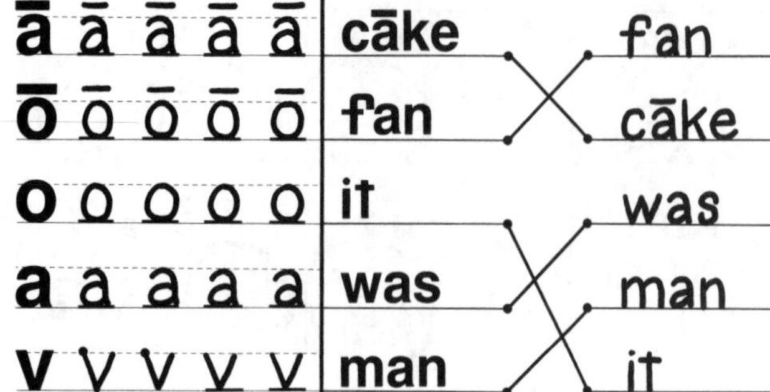

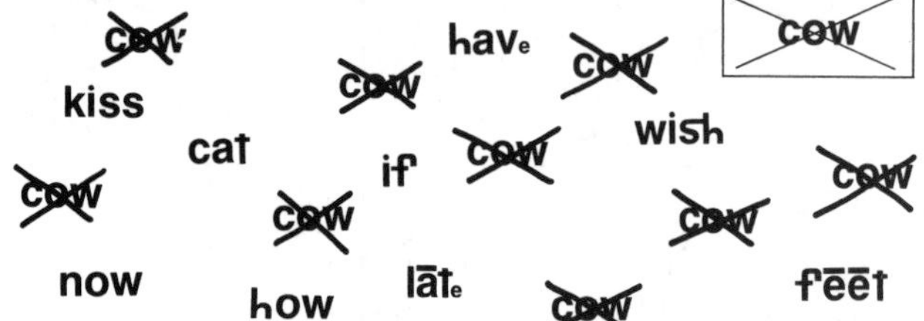

a picture that shows "I can hold the hats."

nōs$_e$	a cat	fat
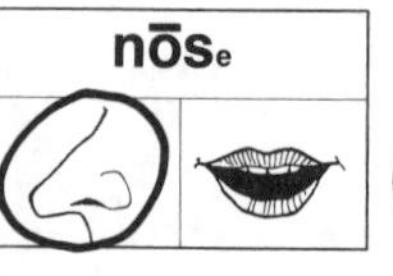		
rag	**mom**	**a dish**
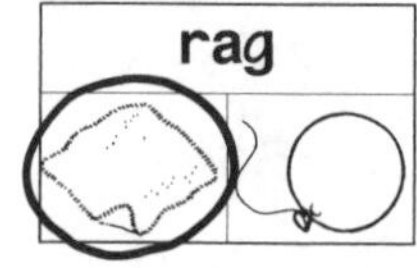		
lāk$_e$	**fēēt**	**tēēth**
	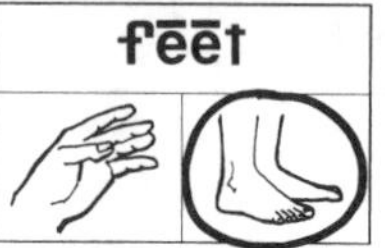	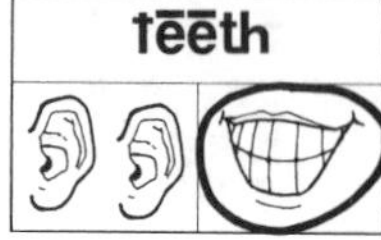
kiss	**a cow**	**lic$_k$**

Printed in the United States of America

NAME ______________________

wē hav$_e$ sac$_k$s.

we have sacks.

we have sacks.

we have sacks.

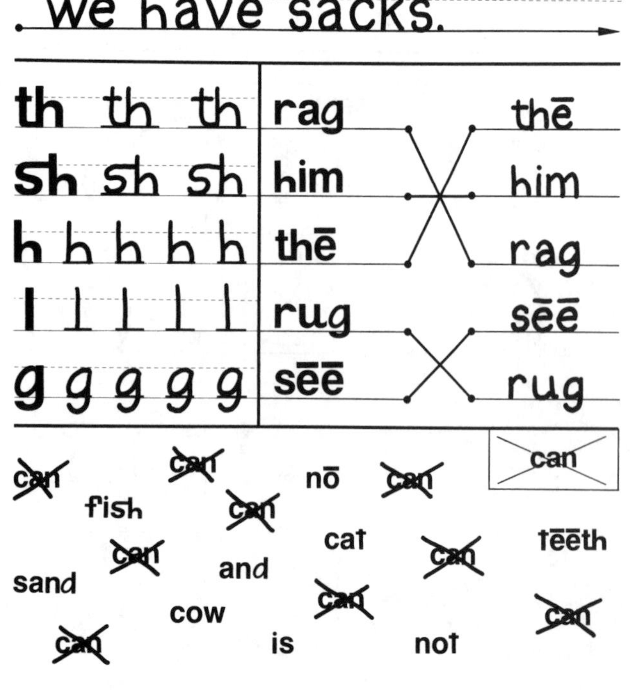

a picture that shows "we have sacks."

kitt$_e$n	hit	ē$_a$rs
		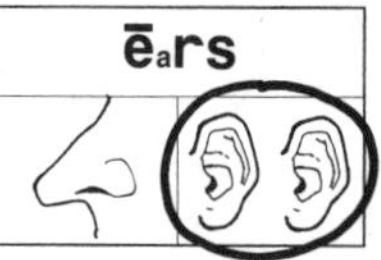
shē	**a sac$_k$**	**sand**

rāk$_e$	**a roc$_k$**	**loc$_k$**
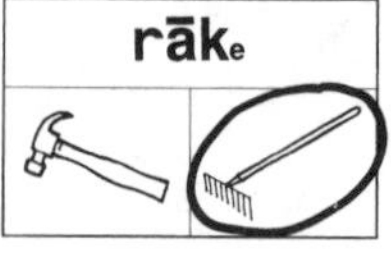		
a rug	**tēēth**	**fan**
	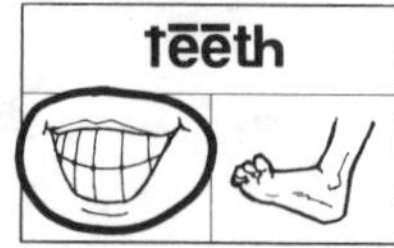	

Printed in the United States of America

NAME ____________________ TAKE-HOME **105** SIDE **1**

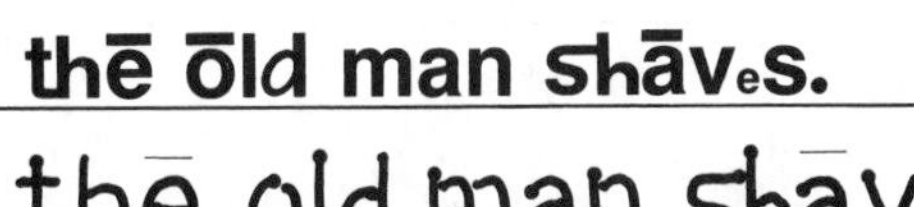

thē ōld man shāvₑs.

the old man shaves.

the old man shaves.

the old man shaves.

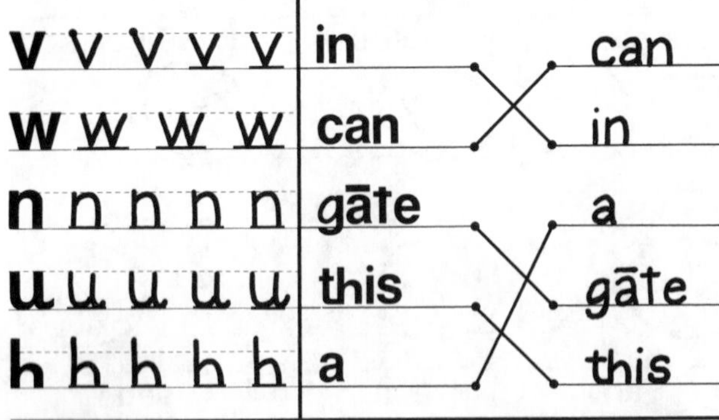

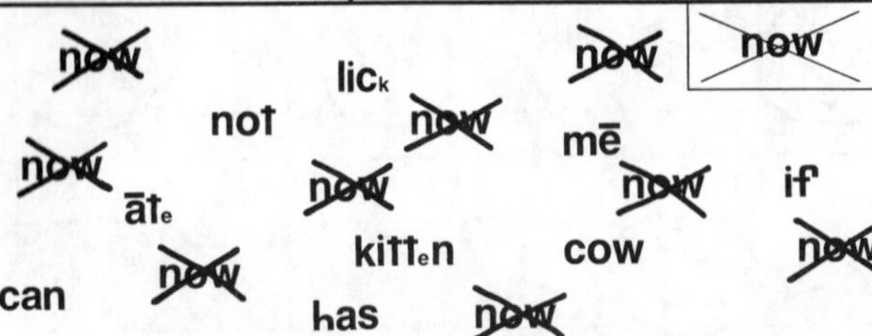

TAKE-HOME **105** SIDE **2**

a picture that shows "the old man shaves."

a cow

lākₑ

hill

mom

kiss

a rocₖ

tēēth

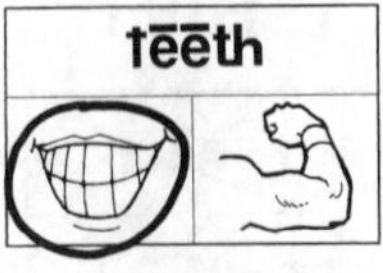

mitt

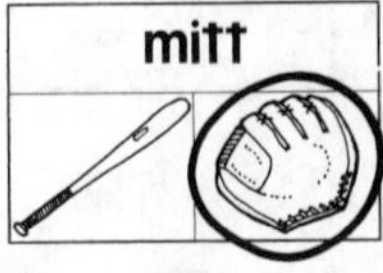

a dish

a fish

nōsₑ

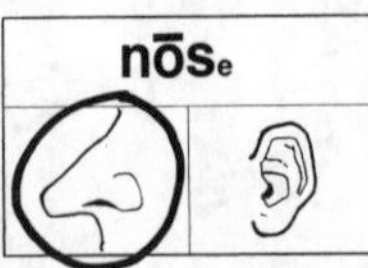

shacₖ

Printed in the United States of America

53

NAME ____________________ TAKE-HOME **106** SIDE **1**

givₑ mē a socₖ.

give me a sock.

give me a sock.

give me a sock.

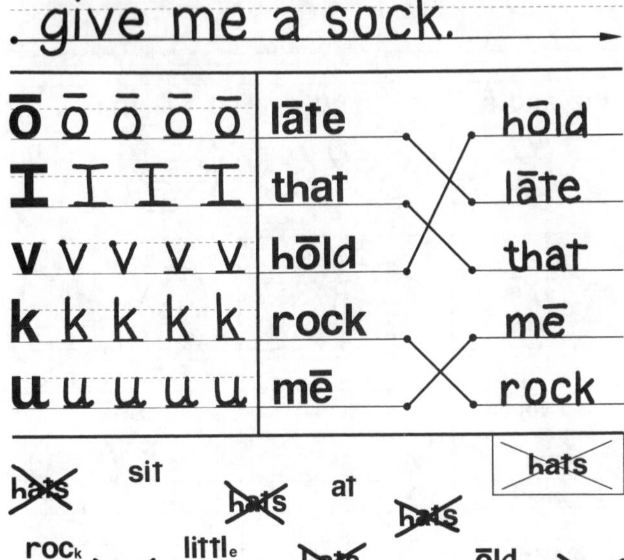

TAKE-HOME **106** SIDE **2**

a picture that shows "give me a sock."

thē hats

ōld

a sacₖ

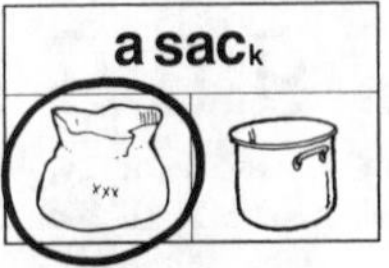

mad

ēₐrs

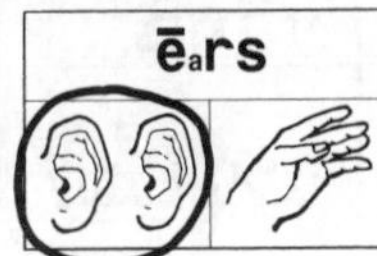

mom

a dish

nōsₑ

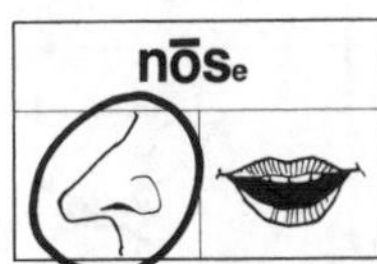

locₖ

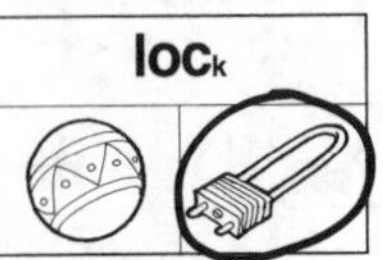

fēēt

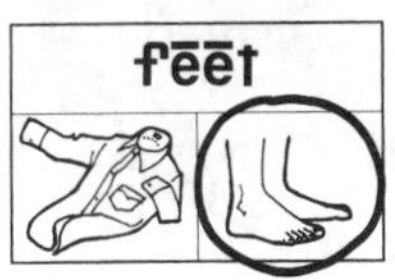

sad

kittₑn

Printed in the United States of America

NAME ______________________

TAKE-HOME 107 SIDE 1

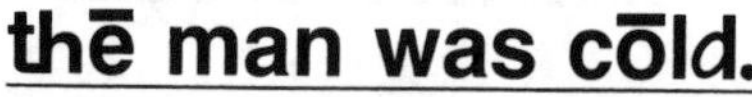

thē man was cōld.

the man was cold.
the man was cold.
the man was cold.

w w w w w	shē	ran
k k k k k	mitt	hats
v v v v v	ran	said
f f f f f	hats	shē
ā ā ā ā ā	said	mitt

will need did need nēēd need need can fēēt sand nō need need tēēth need need hōld need ēat

TAKE-HOME 107 SIDE 2

a picture that shows "the man was cold."

a sack

tēēth
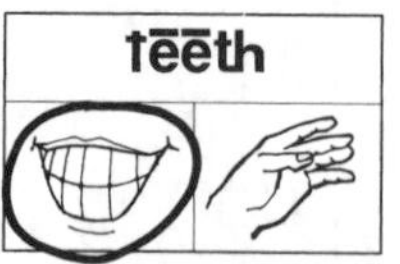

thē rocks

kiss

shē

shack

fan

a man

sand
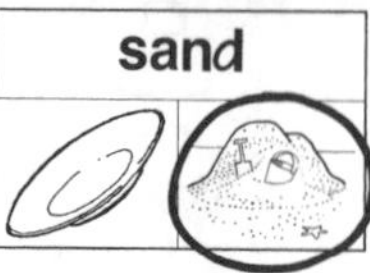

a tāil
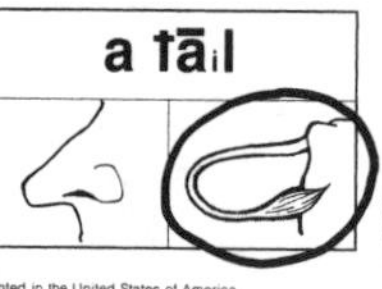

dish

sit

Printed in the United States of America

NAME ______________________

TAKE-HOME 108 SIDE 1

thē gōat āte thē cōat.

the goat ate the coat.
the goat ate the coat.
the goat ate the coat.

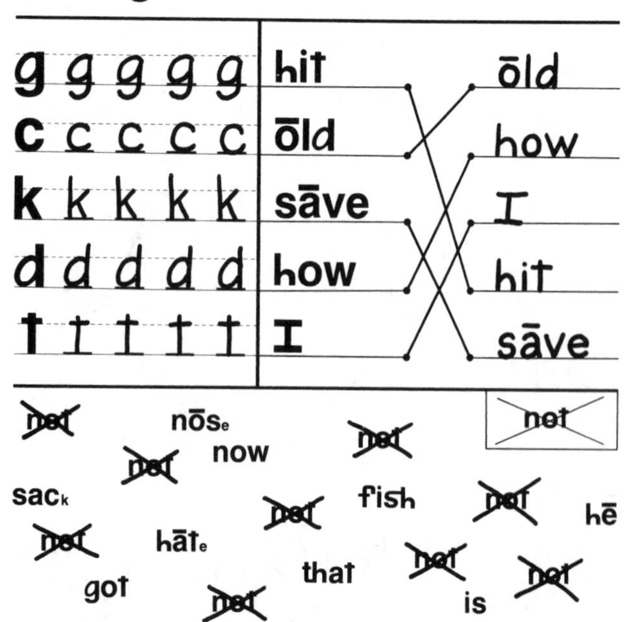

g g g g g	hit	ōld
c c c c c	ōld	how
k k k k k	sāve	I
d d d d d	how	hit
t t t t t	I	sāve

not nōse now not not sack fish not hē not hāte that not not got not is not

TAKE-HOME 108 SIDE 2

A picture that shows "the goat ate his coat."

thē sacks

a rug

tāil
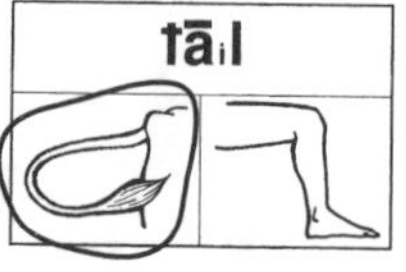

lick

shack

hē

a rāke

nōse
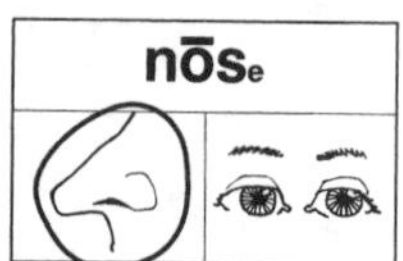

shē

fēēt
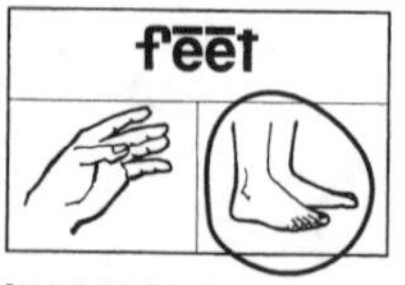

hut

māil
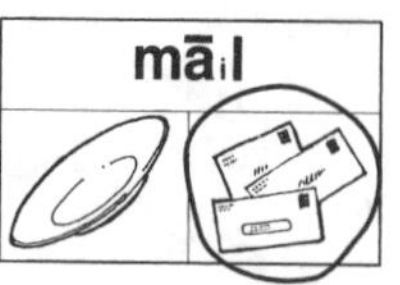

Printed in the United States of America

NAME ____________ TAKE-HOME 109 SIDE 1

a cow got on a rock.

a cow got on a rock.

a cow got on a rock.

a cow got on a rock.

p p p p p	sat		mud
v v v v v	hē		sat
d d d d d	now		hē
g g g g g	mud		nāme
s s s s s	nāme		now

man

on man man said man not man sand man man shāve man man sō mad rock man man nēēd

TAKE-HOME 109 SIDE 2

a picture that shows "a cow got on a rock."

shack	ēars	hut
	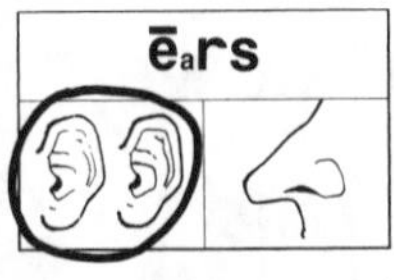	
a fish	**him**	**ōld**

lāke	**a mitt**	**a sack**

mom	**fēēt**	**a cow**
	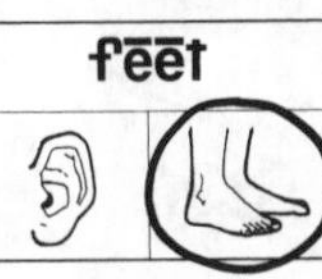	

NAME ____________ TAKE-HOME 110 SIDE 1

hē had sand on him.

he had sand on him.

he had sand on him.

he had sand on him.

p p p p p	sock		ham
g g g g g	of		to
v v v v v	run		sock
t t t t t	ham		of
I I I I I	to		run

sand

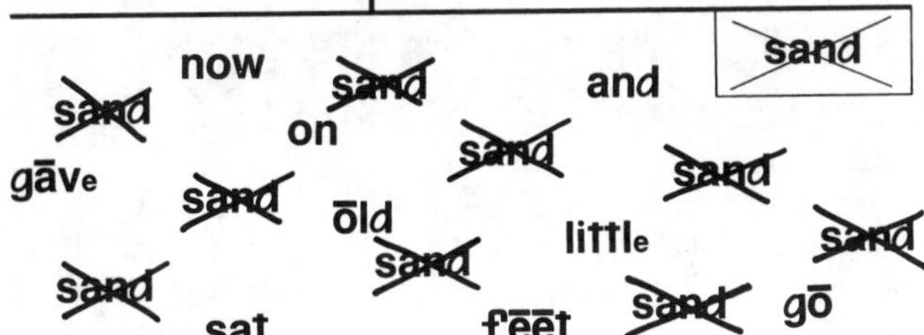

TAKE-HOME 110 SIDE 2

a picture that shows "he had sand on him."

a cōat	hill	lock
		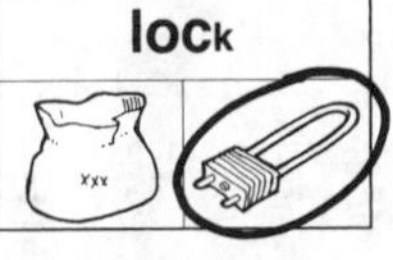
a tāil	**tēēth**	**a dish**
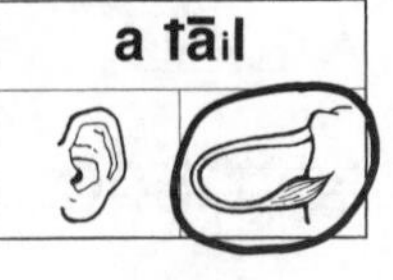	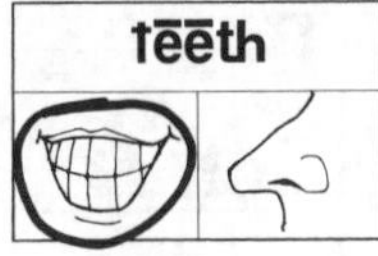	
nōse	**hut**	**gōat**
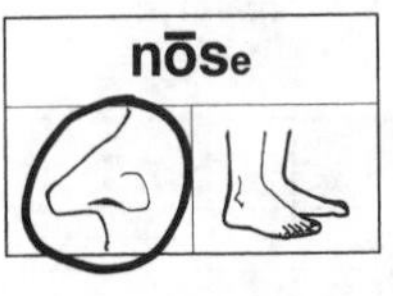		
shē	**a rāke**	**cōld**
	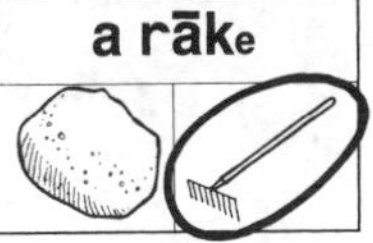	

NAME ____________________ TAKE-HOME 111 SIDE 1

hē ran thē fan.

hē ran thē fan.

he ran the fan.

he ran the fan.

sh sh sh	cow	ēat
th th th	did	cow
o o o o o	lock	lock
ō ō ō ō ō	ēat	did
v v v v v	mom	mom

~~run~~

~~run~~ sō ~~run~~ ~~run~~ ~~run~~ is fun ~~run~~ lāte rag ~~run~~ ~~run~~ ~~run~~ ~~run~~ sand did got rug

TAKE-HOME 111 SIDE 2

a picture that shows "he ran the fan."

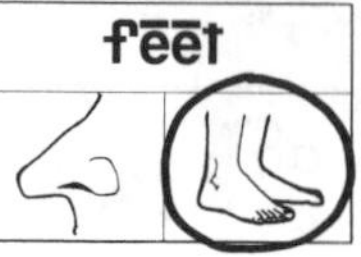

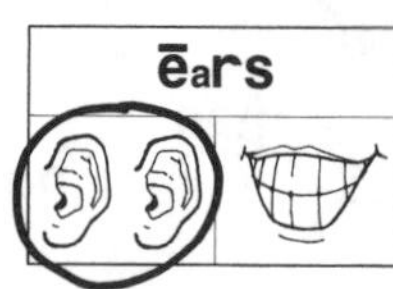

Printed in the United States of America

NAME ____________________ TAKE-HOME 112 SIDE 1

thē dog āte thē car.

thē dog āte thē car.

the dog ate the car.

the dog ate the car.

r r r r r	fun	fun
sh sh sh	give	and
ē ē ē ē ē	māde	give
u u u u u	lick	māde
l l l l l	and	lick

~~hand~~

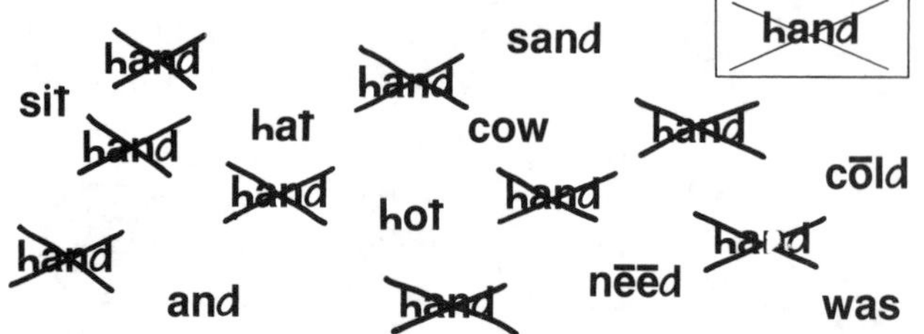

TAKE-HOME 112 SIDE 2

A picture that shows "the dog ate the car."

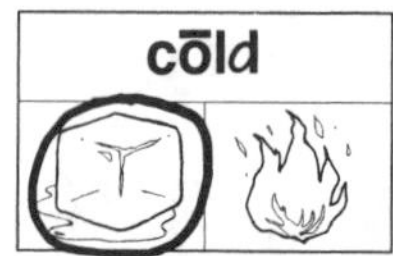

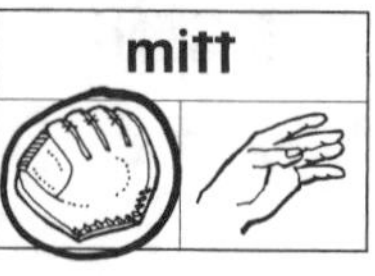

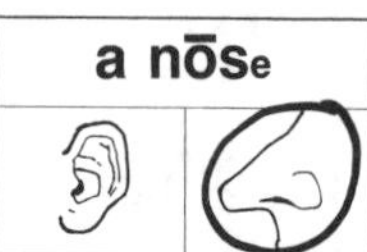

Printed in the United States of America

NAME ____________ TAKE-HOME 113 SIDE 1

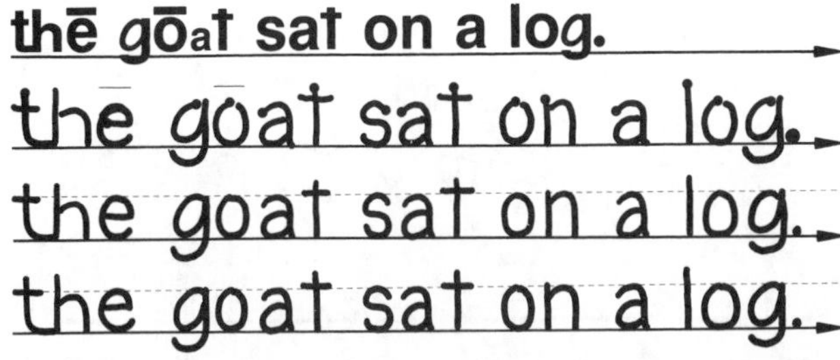

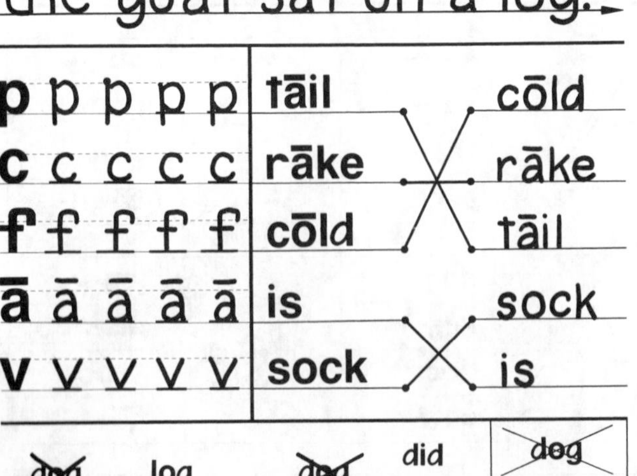

dog log dog did dog
gāte dog nō dog dog
dog said
dish dog shāve dog
dog cow hē

TAKE-HOME 113 SIDE 2

A picture that shows
"the goat sat on a log."

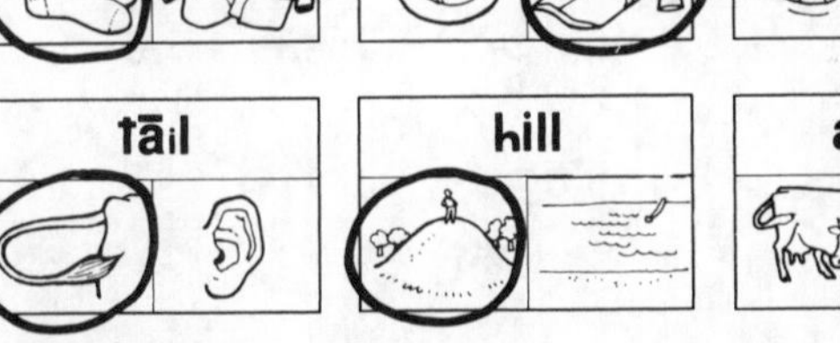

NAME ____________ TAKE-HOME 114 SIDE 1

a man sat on a gōat.
a man sat on a goat.
a man sat on a goat.
a man sat on a goat.

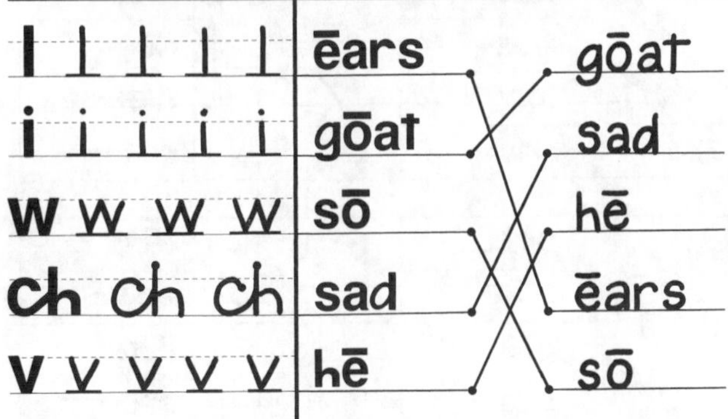

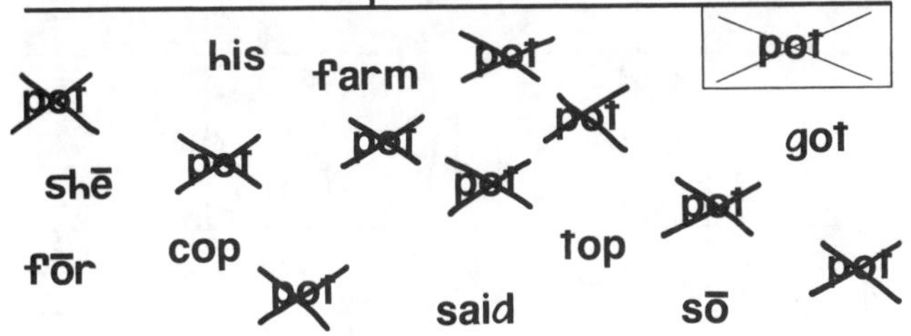

TAKE-HOME 114 SIDE 2

A picture that shows
"a man sat on a goat."

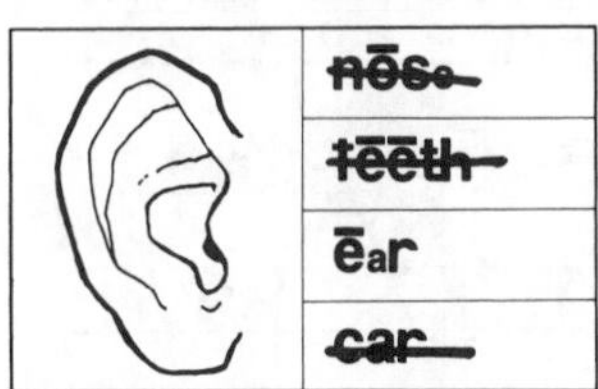

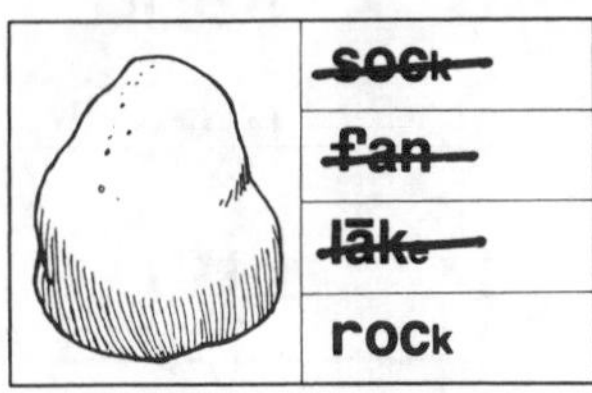

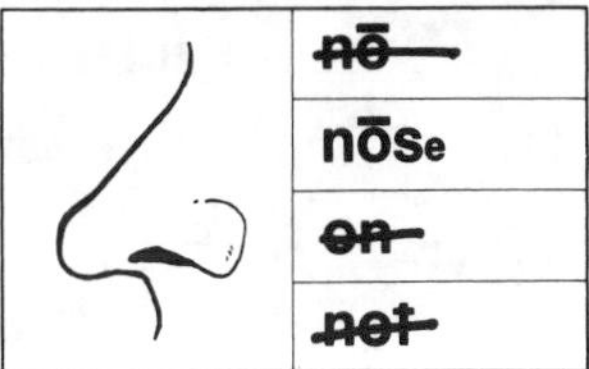

NAME ________________ TAKE-HOME 115 SIDE 1

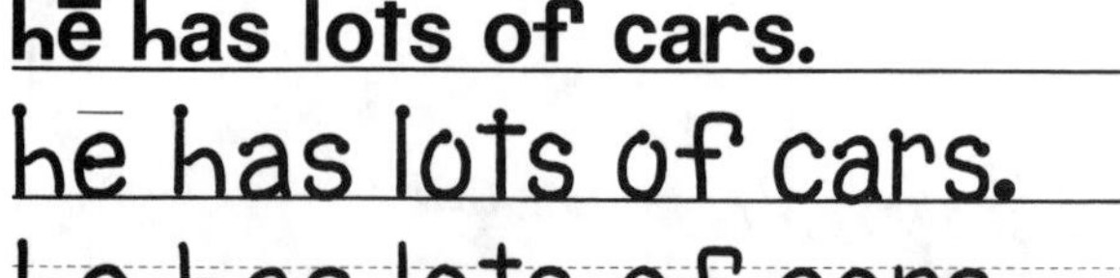

hē has lots of cars.

he has lots of cars.

he has lots of cars.

he has lots of cars.

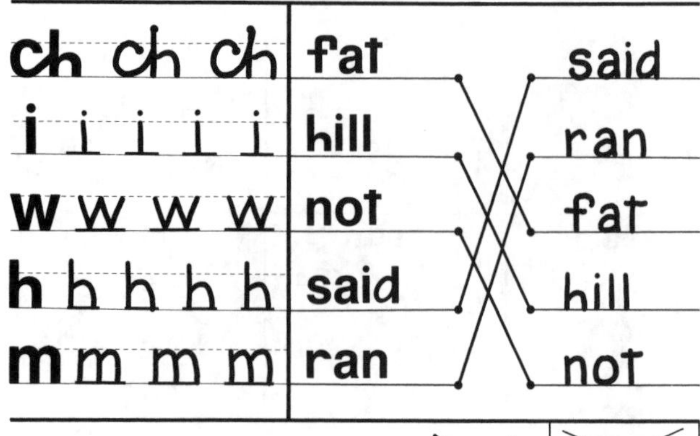

ch ch ch	fat	said
i i i i i	hill	ran
w w w w	not	fat
h h h h h	said	hill
m m m m	ran	not

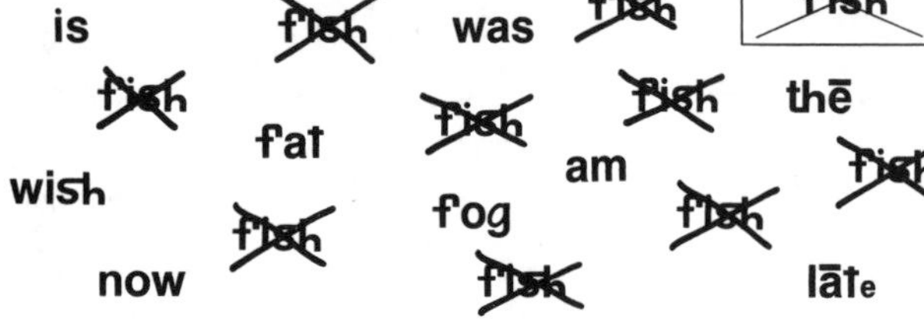

is ~~fish~~ was ~~fish~~ ~~fish~~

~~fish~~ fat ~~fish~~ ~~fish~~ thē

wish am ~~fish~~

~~fish~~ fog ~~fish~~

now ~~fish~~ lāte

TAKE-HOME 115 SIDE 2

A picture that shows "he has lots of cars."

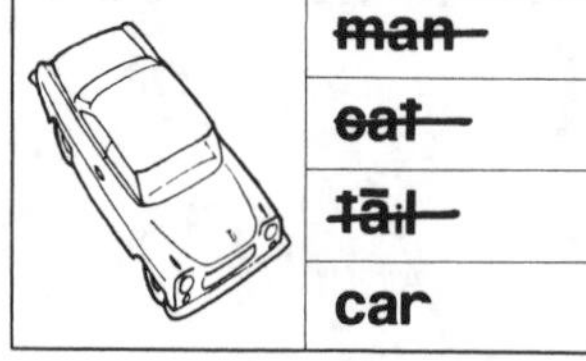

~~man~~ / ~~eat~~ / ~~tāil~~ / car

~~rug~~ / rat / ~~gāte~~ / ~~rāke~~

dog / ~~rag~~ / ~~rock~~ / ~~cow~~

~~log~~ / ~~dish~~ / shack / ~~gōat~~

cōat / ~~ean~~ / ~~cōld~~ / ~~car~~

~~tāil~~ / ~~āte~~ / māil / ~~shāve~~

Printed in the United States of America

NAME ________________ TAKE-HOME 116 SIDE 1

thē dog said, "nō."

the dog said, "no."

the dog said, "no."

the dog said, "no."

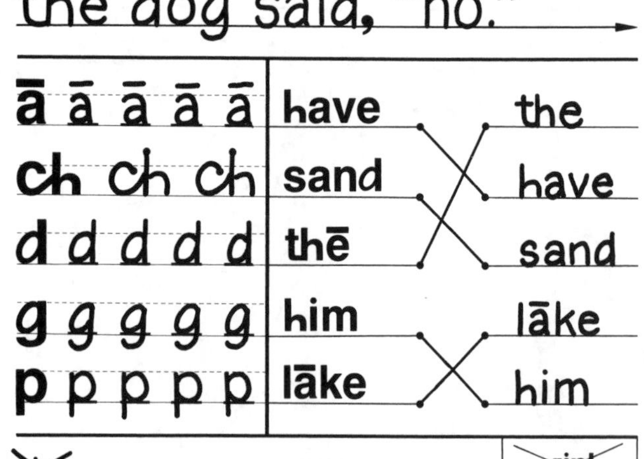

ā ā ā ā ā	have	the
ch ch ch	sand	have
d d d d d	thē	sand
g g g g g	him	lāke
p p p p p	lāke	him

~~girl~~ if said sack ~~girl~~ ~~girl~~

~~girl~~ log

not ~~girl~~ sō ~~girl~~

~~girl~~ ~~girl~~ ~~girl~~

gōat fēet ~~girl~~ sand

TAKE-HOME 116 SIDE 2

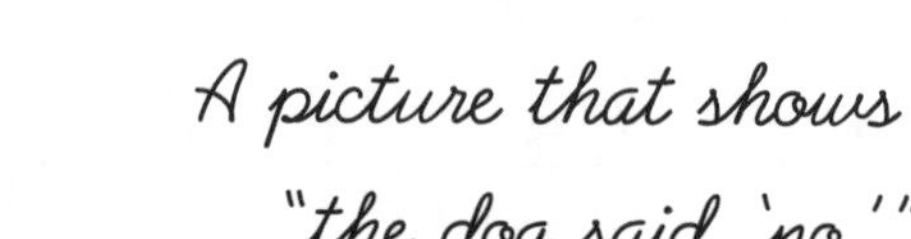

A picture that shows "the dog said, 'no.'"

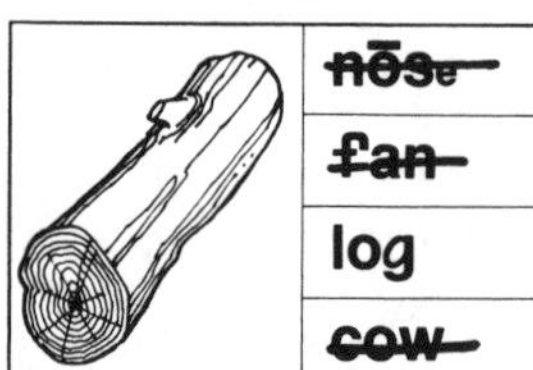

~~nōse~~ / ~~fan~~ / log / ~~cow~~

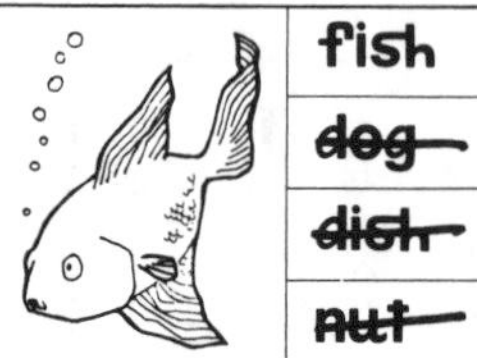

fish / ~~dog~~ / ~~dish~~ / ~~nut~~

~~pot~~ / gōat / ~~gāte~~ / ~~gun~~

~~tāil~~ / ~~rock~~ / lāke / ~~sack~~

~~sad~~ / sand / ~~and~~ / ~~fan~~

sēat / ~~fēet~~ / ~~shē~~ / ~~said~~

Printed in the United States of America

NAME ______________________ TAKE-HOME 117 SIDE 1

a girl was in a cāve.

a girl was in a cave.

a girl was in a cave.

a girl was in a cave.

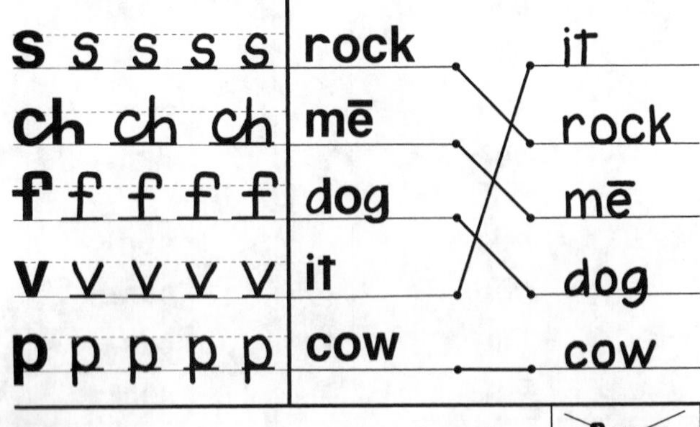

s s s s s	rock	it
ch ch ch	mē	rock
f f f f f	dog	mē
v v v v v	it	dog
p p p p p	cow	cow

~~farm~~

gōat, sit, ~~farm~~, hand, ~~farm~~, ~~farm~~, ~~farm~~, ~~farm~~, said, hē, ~~farm~~, ~~farm~~, ~~farm~~, ōld, little, ~~farm~~, run, now

TAKE-HOME 117 SIDE 2

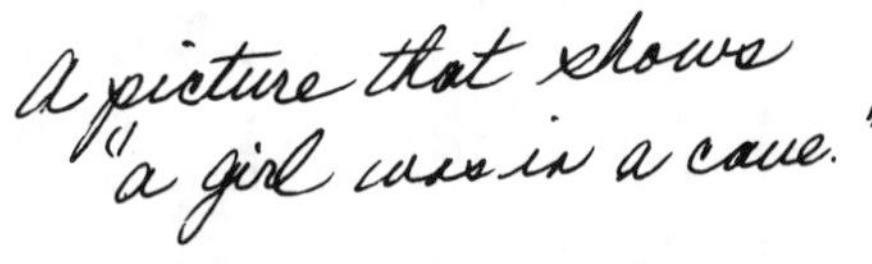

~~hē~~
~~fish~~
~~man~~
shē

~~mad~~
fat
~~sad~~
~~mēan~~

lock
~~cōat~~
~~sack~~
~~hut~~

~~log~~
~~mom~~
nōse
~~fēet~~

~~ran~~
rōad
~~dog~~
~~car~~

~~āte~~
~~rock~~
gāte
~~fish~~

Printed in the United States of America

59

NAME ______________________ TAKE-HOME 118 SIDE 1

hē has lots of pots.

he has lots of pots.

he has lots of pots.

he has lots of pots.

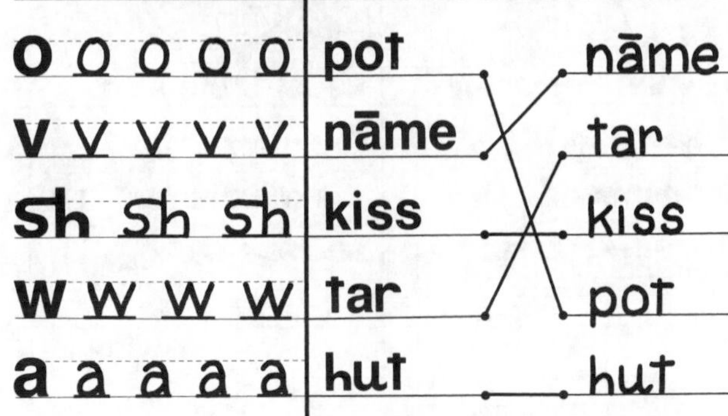

o o o o o	pot	nāme
v v v v v	nāme	tar
sh sh sh	kiss	kiss
w w w w w	tar	pot
a a a a a	hut	hut

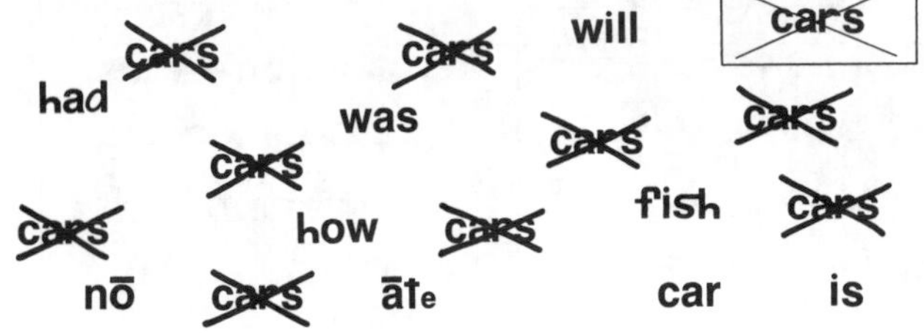

~~cars~~

~~cars~~, ~~cars~~, will, had, was, ~~cars~~, ~~cars~~, ~~cars~~, fish, ~~cars~~, ~~cars~~, how, ~~cars~~, nō, ~~cars~~, āte, car, is

TAKE-HOME 118 SIDE 2

~~hat~~
cōat
~~rug~~
~~dog~~

cat
~~fish~~
~~cow~~
~~gōat~~

~~fish~~
~~pot~~
dish
~~ship~~

~~ear~~
~~rag~~
~~log~~
pot

~~fat~~
~~cow~~
~~car~~
farm

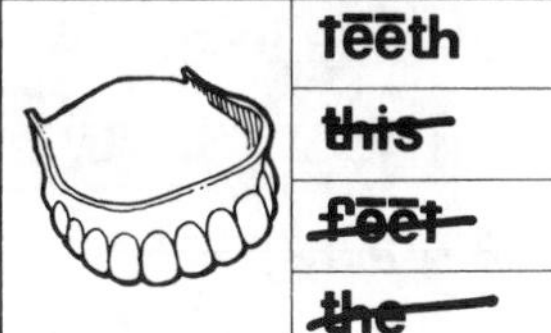

tēeth
~~this~~
~~fēet~~
~~the~~

Printed in the United States of America

NAME

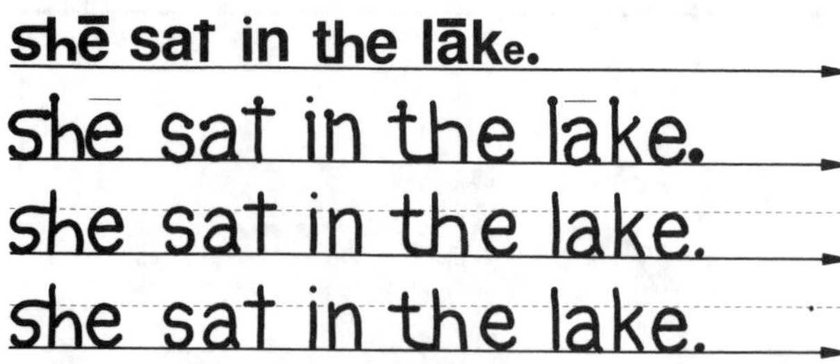

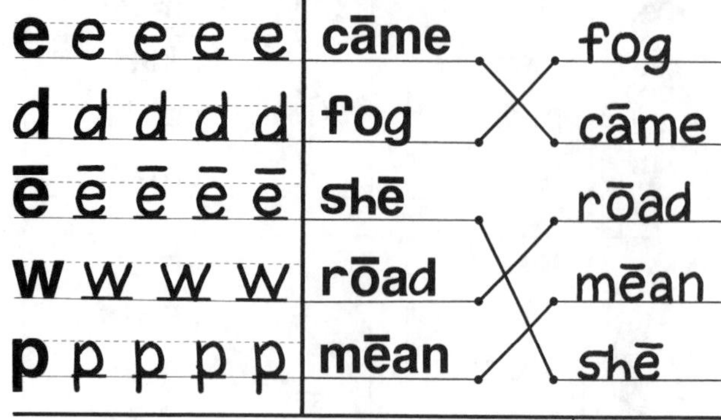

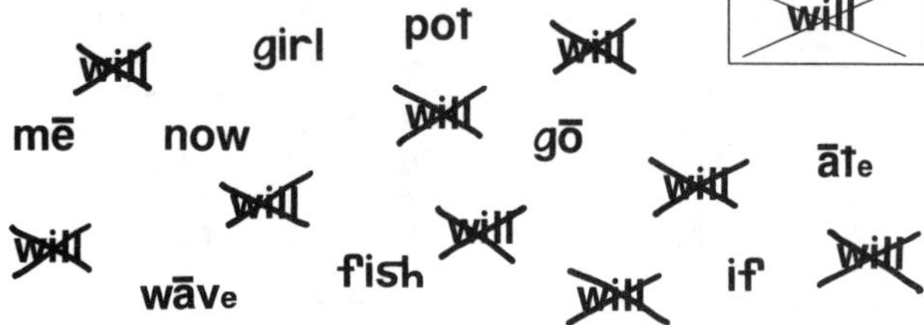

a picture that shows "she sat in the lake."

~~eat~~
girl
~~man~~
~~pot~~

rōad
~~gāte~~
~~lāke~~
~~dish~~

~~nōse~~
~~fēēt~~
tāil
~~ēars~~

~~cop~~
~~sand~~
~~car~~
sack

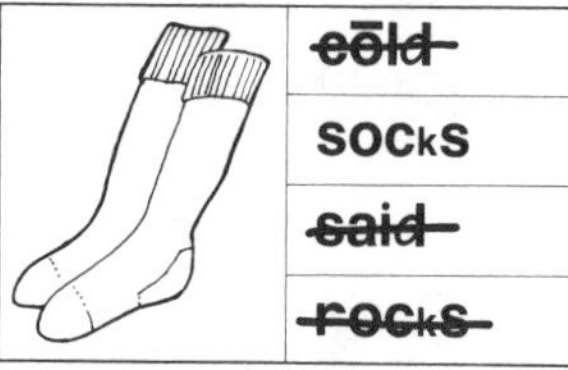

~~cōld~~
socks
~~said~~
~~rocks~~

rāke
~~cāke~~
~~cat~~
~~hōld~~

Printed in the United States of America

NAME

A picture that shows this sentence

the girl got wet.
the girl got wet.
the girl got wet.

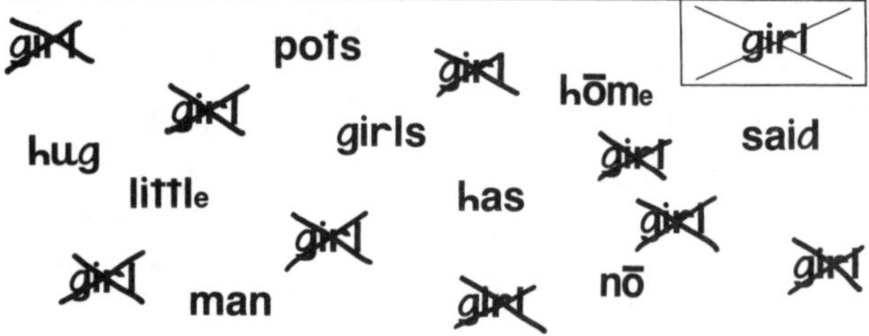

ron was in the rāin.
hē got wet.

1. ron was in the...
   - rat
   - (rāin)
   - sand
2. hē got...
   - fat
   - sick
   - (wet)

e e e e e e | p p p p p p
d d d d d d | w w w w w
g g g g g g | I I I I I

~~the man has a sack.~~
hē has a mitt.
~~sam is mad.~~
~~hē made a fuss.~~

hē is in the sun.
~~it is in the mud.~~
~~the man is not fat.~~
~~hē āte a nut.~~

~~I am on the log.~~
~~wē will ēat fish.~~
hē is in a car.
~~hē has a fan.~~

~~a rat is on a rug.~~
~~hē sat on a rock.~~
~~wē have sand.~~
a girl has a gōat.

Printed in the United States of America

NAME

A picture that shows this sentence

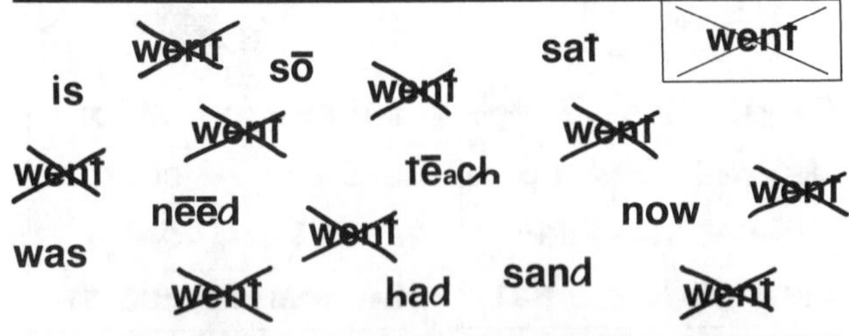

the girl got a cat.
the girl got a cat.
the girl got a cat.

~~went~~ is ~~went~~ sō sat ~~went~~ ~~went~~ ~~went~~ tēach ~~went~~ nēēd now ~~went~~ was ~~went~~ had sand ~~went~~ ~~went~~ ~~went~~

the girl went to a shop.
shē got a cat.

1. the girl went to a...
   - ship
   - car
   - shop

2. shē got a...
   - cat
   - dog
   - car

d d d d d d | n n n n n n
e e e e e e | s s s s s s
p p p p p p | r r r r r r

~~that man is mōan.~~
a girl has a sack.
~~a man will ēat ham.~~
~~hē āte a fig.~~

the man has a cow.
~~hē is in the mud.~~
~~a girl has a fan.~~
~~a nut is on a log.~~

~~the girl can run.~~
~~hē has the māil.~~
shē has a pot.
~~wē will sit in sand.~~

~~shē ran and ran.~~
this cat is fat.
~~wē lock the nut.~~
~~a man is in a shack.~~

Printed in the United States of America

NAME

A picture that shows this sentence

the cow sat in a car.
the cow sat in a car.
the cow sat in a car.

~~pet~~ sat pets ~~pet~~ wish ~~pet~~ pot said ~~pet~~ gō ~~pet~~ dog ~~pet~~ ~~pet~~ ~~pet~~ ~~pet~~ ~~pet~~ the nō

the cow was on the rōad.
the men got mad.

1. the cow was on the...
   - car
   - rōad
   - farm

2. the men got...
   - sad
   - māde
   - mad

t t t t t t | u u u u u u
d d d d d d | I I I I I
p p p p p p | ch ch ch ch

~~a cat has fat fēēt.~~
~~hē will ēat fish.~~
shē is in the mud.
~~a gōat is on a car.~~

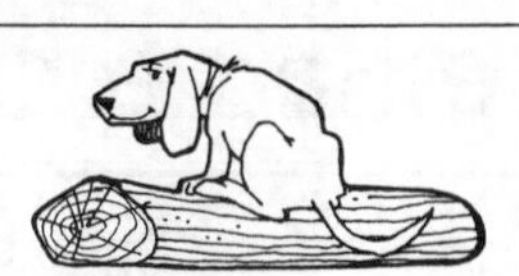

~~hē has a pot.~~
~~a gōat āte a sock.~~
~~wē are not sad.~~
the dog is on a log.

~~his cat is fat.~~
shē has the māil.
~~hē has a shack.~~
~~sam āte cōrn.~~

this man is ōld.
~~his fēēt are wet.~~
~~shē is in a car.~~
~~that dog is mad.~~

Printed in the United States of America

NAME ______________________ TAKE-HOME 123 SIDE 1

A picture that shows this sentence

it is fun to pet pigs.

it is fun to pet pigs.

it is fun to pet pigs.

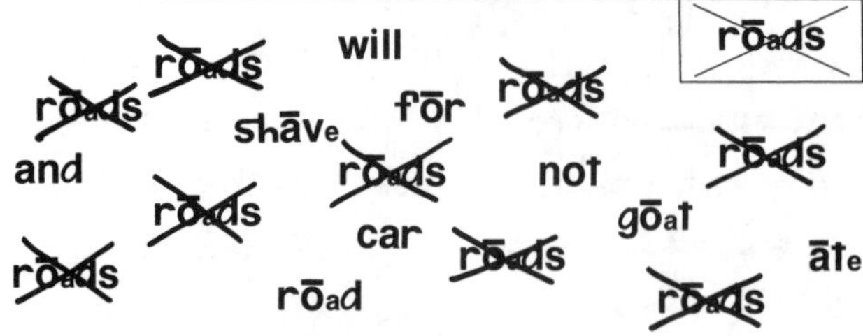

~~rōads~~ will ~~rōads~~ fōr ~~rōads~~ shāve ~~rōads~~ and ~~rōads~~ not ~~rōads~~ ~~rōads~~ car gōat ~~rōads~~ ~~rōads~~ āte rōad ~~rōads~~

the gōat went to the park.
the girl went to the farm.

1. the gōat went...
   - in a car • in the rāin • (to the park)
2. the girl went to the...
   - car • (farm) • park

TAKE-HOME 123 SIDE 2

d d d d d d | m m m m m
w w w w w | h h h h h h
f f f f f | l l l l l l

~~the pot has nō top.~~
~~shē will fēēd a pig.~~
~~shē sat in a lāke.~~
the fish has a hat.

~~wē are on a ship.~~
shē will ēat cōrn.
~~now I am cōld.~~
~~the man has socks.~~

~~the girl can run.~~
~~a cōat is in mud.~~
mom has a sock.
~~that is his dog.~~

~~his fēēt got hot.~~
~~shē is on a hill.~~
~~I will run.~~
hē sat on a gāte.

Printed in the United States of America.

NAME ______________________ TAKE-HOME 124 SIDE 1

A picture that shows this sentence

he had a red nose.

he had a red nose.

he had a red nose.

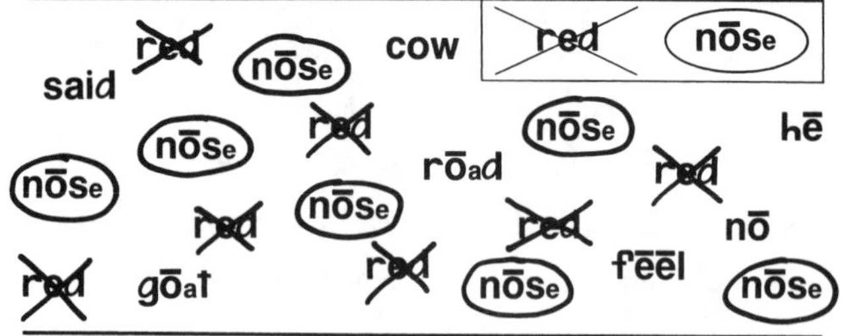

~~red~~ (nōse) said ~~red~~ (nōse) cow (nōse) ~~red~~ (nōse) hē (nōse) rōad ~~red~~ ~~red~~ (nōse) ~~red~~ nō ~~red~~ gōat ~~red~~ (nōse) fēēl (nōse)

the little dog had a red nōse.
hē was mad.

1. the little dog had a...
   - big nōse • hot nōse • (red nōse)
2. hē was...
   - sad • (mad) • big

TAKE-HOME 124 SIDE 2

b b b b b b | t t t t t t
ā ā ā ā ā ā | c c c c c c
g g g g g g | i i i i i i

~~shē can kick.~~
~~I am not a fish.~~
the gōat āte a hat.
~~wē are in the rāin.~~

~~wē can gō in a car.~~
~~shē will kiss him.~~
hē has a big fish.
~~I fēēd the cat.~~

~~his ēars are little.~~
~~shē sat with a cat.~~
mom has a rāke.
~~hē will ēat cāke.~~

~~hē sat on a log.~~
the man has a cow.
~~shē has nō tēēth.~~
~~this rat is fat.~~

Printed in the United States of America.

NAME ____________

A picture that shows this sentence

she got a red hat.
she got a red hat.
she got a red hat.

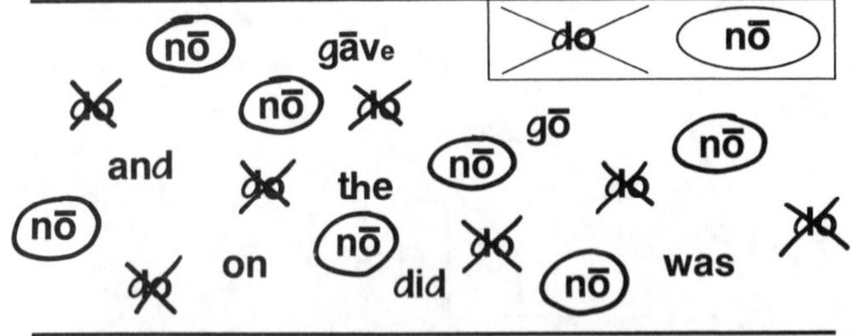

the fish got a hat.
the cow got a car.

1. the fish got...
•a hat •a gōat •a fish

2. the cow got a...
•cat •car •cow

d d d d d d | c c c c c c
b b b b b b | ē ē ē ē ē ē
g g g g g g | r r r r r r

a cow can lick mē.
the girl got wet.
hē has a hat.
I have cōrn.

wē will ēat cōrn.
I am not fat.
a man is on a rōad.
shē has socks.

hē has a gōat.
the girl is cōld.
shē ran in the sand.
that dog is mad.

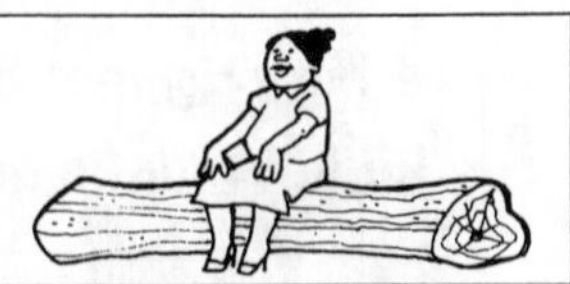

a dog is in a car.
shē sat on a log.
that is a cop.
I can run.

Printed in the United States of America

NAME ____________

A picture that shows this sentence

the bug bit the log.
the bug bit the log.
the bug bit the log.

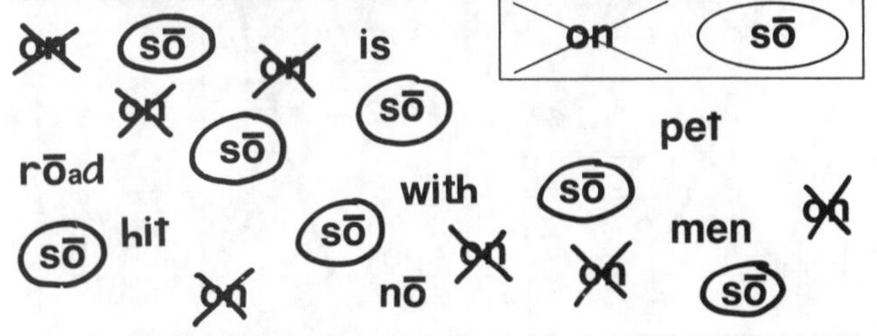

the bug got mad.
sō shē bit a log.

1. the bug...
•got big •got mad •got sad

2. sō shē bit a...
•dog •lock •log

sh sh sh sh | ā ā ā ā ā ā
o o o o o o | v v v v v v
b b b b b b | p p p p p p

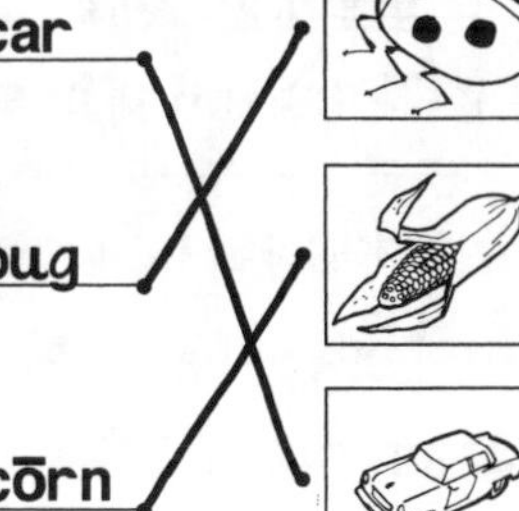

Printed in the United States of America

NAME ______________________ TAKE-HOME 127 SIDE 1

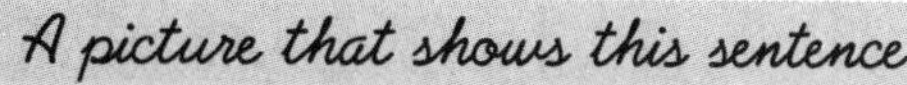

she ate the log.
she ate the log.
she ate the log.

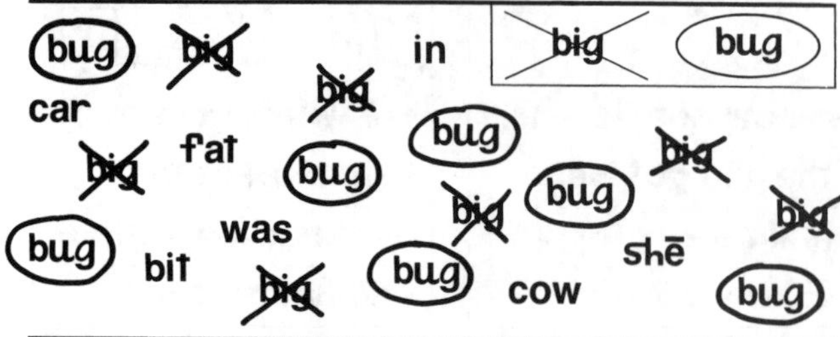

a big bug met a little bug.
hē said, "let's gō ēat."

1. a big bug met a little...
 •big •dog •bug

2. hē said, "let's gō..."
 •hōme •ēat •slēēp

TAKE-HOME 127 SIDE 2

I I I I I | ō ō ō ō ō ō
b b b b b b | ch ch ch ch
k k k k k k | h h h h h h

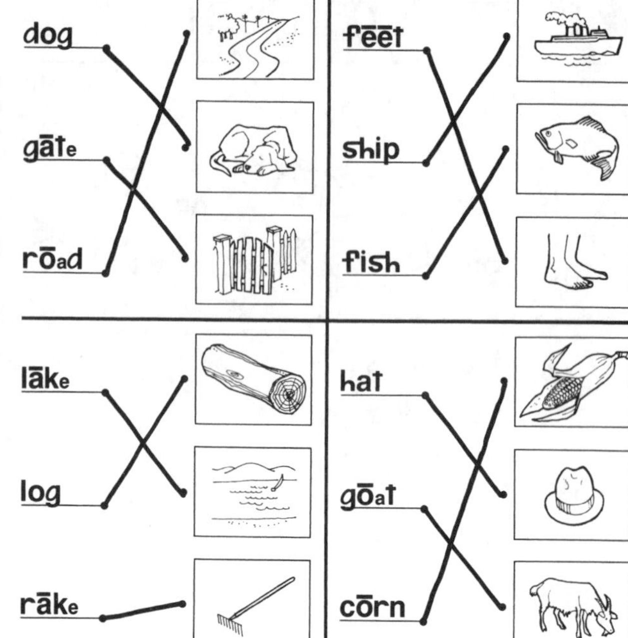

Printed in the United States of America

NAME ______________________ TAKE-HOME 128 SIDE 1

A picture that shows this sentence

the bug was on a dog.
the bug was on a dog.
the bug was on a dog.

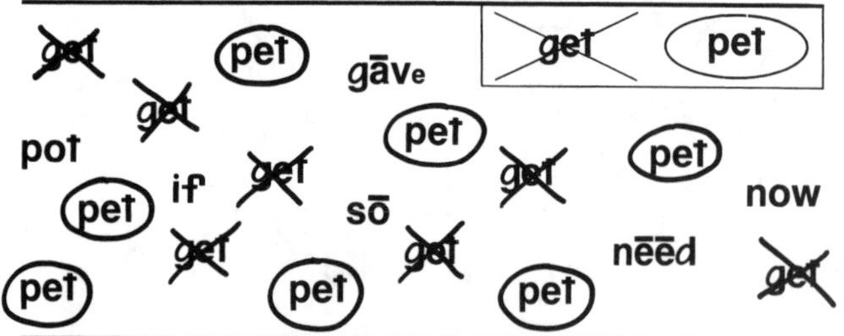

the dog said, "I am a dog.
I am not a bus."

1. the dog said, "I am a...
 •log •frog •dog

2. I am not a..."
 •bug •bus •bēē

TAKE-HOME 128 SIDE 2

b b b b b b | ē ē ē ē ē ē
e e e e e e | I I I I I I
ch ch ch ch | th th th th

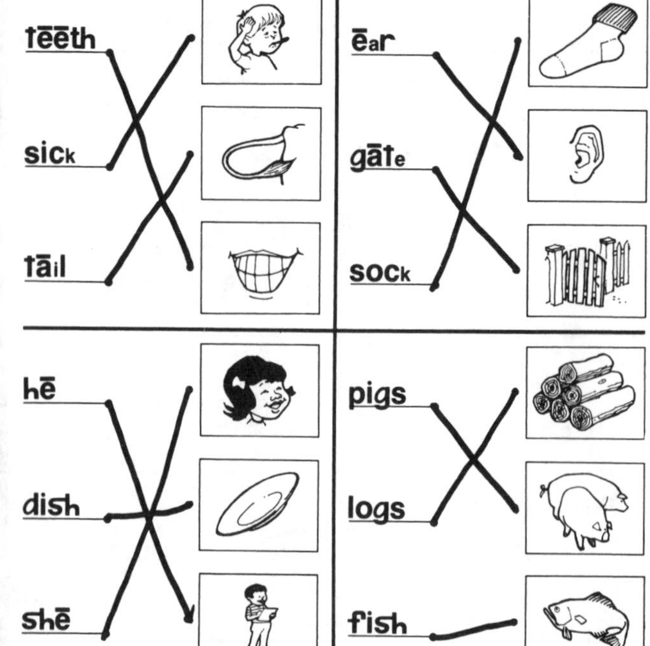

Printed in the United States of America

A picture that shows this sentence

a man had a tub.
a man had a tub.
a man had a tub.

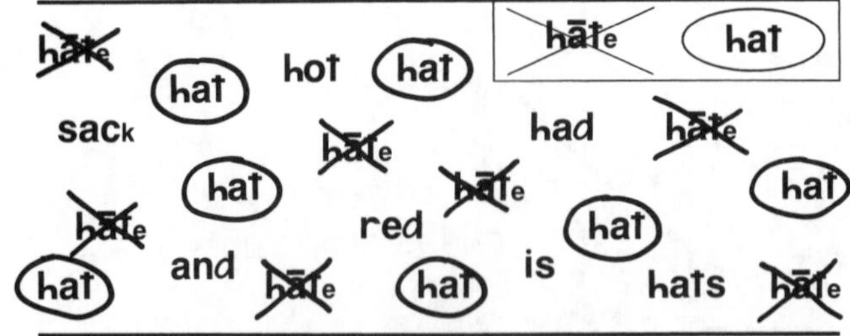

hāte hat

the man had a tub.
hē said, "I līke to rub, rub."

1. the man had a...
   - tub
   - top
   - bug

2. hē said, "I līke to..."
   - run, run
   - rēad, rēad
   - rub, rub

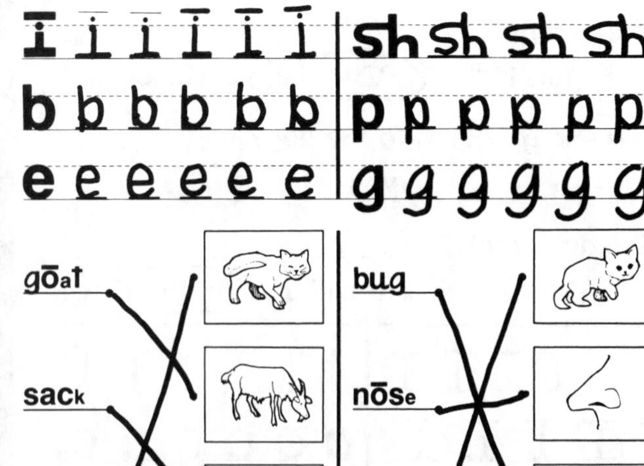

gōat, sack, cat

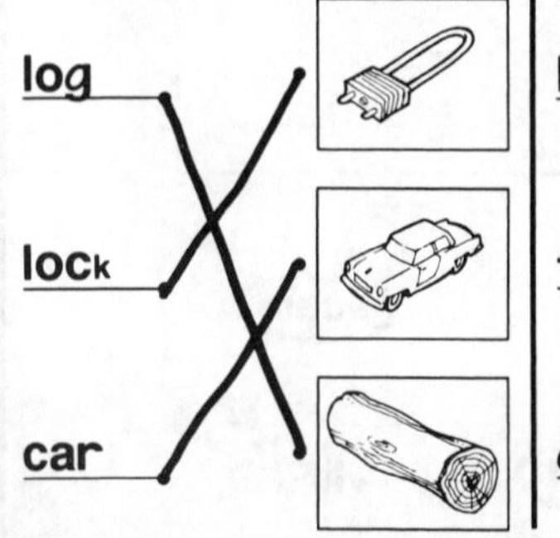

bug, nōse, kitten

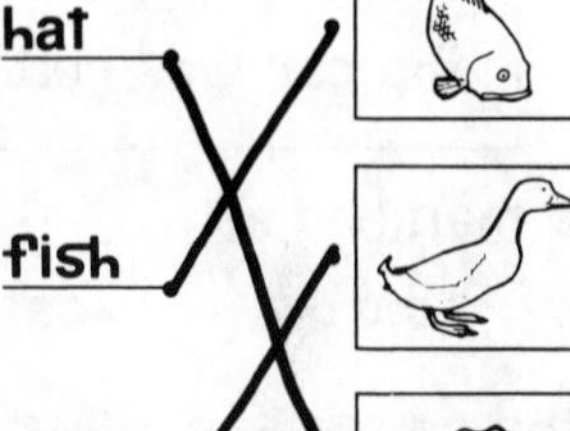

log, lock, car

hat, fish, duck

Printed in the United States of America

A picture that shows this sentence

she met a fat cat.
she met a fat cat.
she met a fat cat.

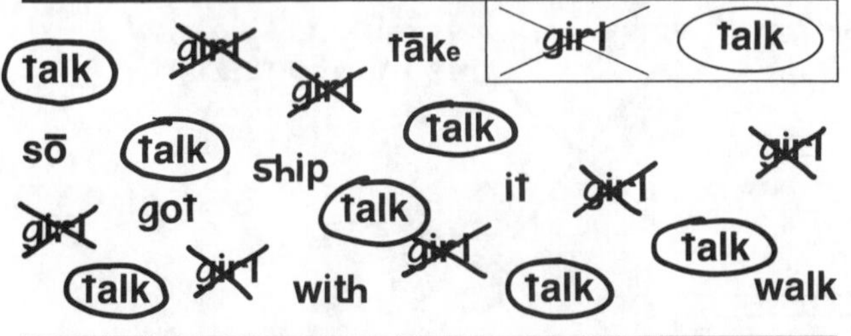

girl talk

"can cats talk?" the girl said.
the cat said, "I can talk."

1. "can cats talk?" the...
   - man said
   - girl said
   - gōat said

2. the cat said, "I can..."
   - talk
   - run
   - wish

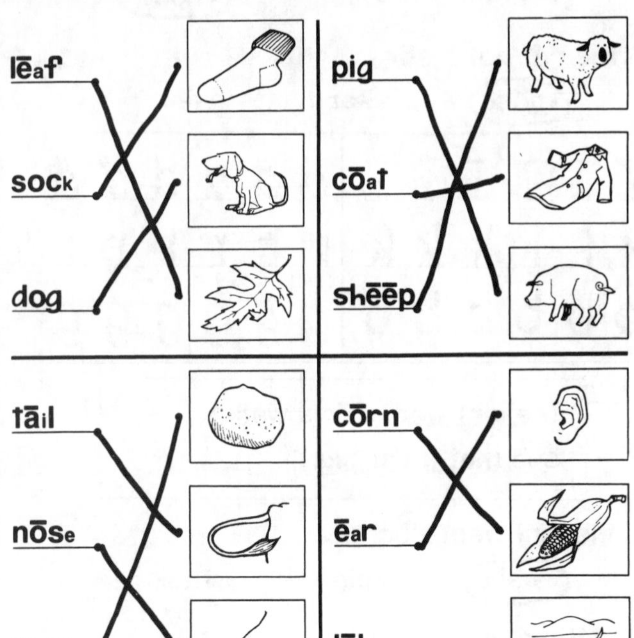

lēaf, sock, dog

pig, cōat, shēēp

tāil, nōse, rock

cōrn, ēar, lāke

Printed in the United States of America

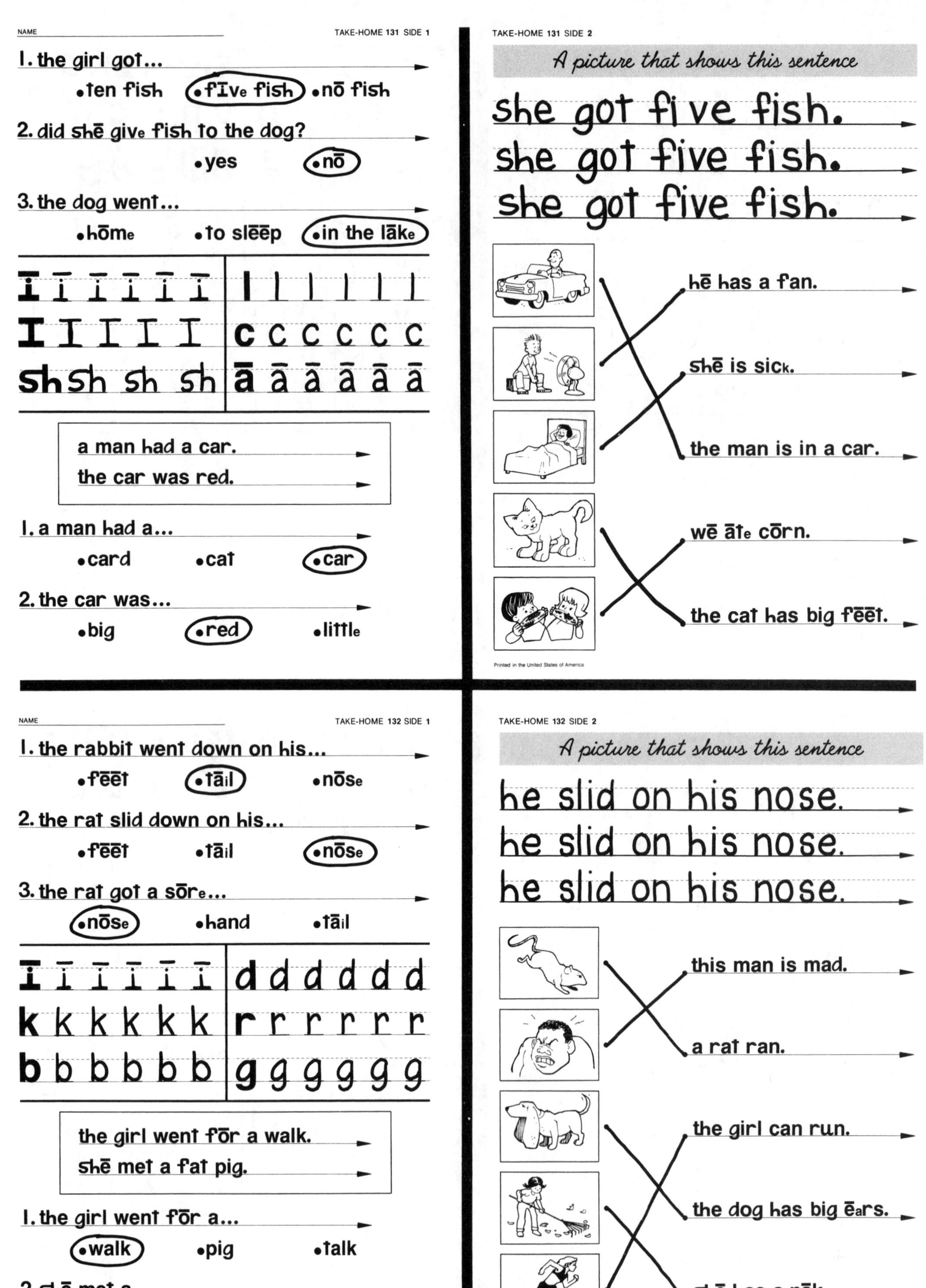

NAME ______

TAKE-HOME 131 SIDE 1

1. the girl got...

• ten fish   **• fīve fish**   • nō fish

2. did shē give fish to the dog?

• yes   **• nō**

3. the dog went...

• hōme   • to slēēp   **• in the lāke**

ī ī ī ī ī ī | l l l l l l
I I I I I | c c c c c c
sh sh sh sh | ā ā ā ā ā ā

a man had a car.
the car was red.

1. a man had a...

• card   • cat   **• car**

2. the car was...

• big   **• red**   • little

TAKE-HOME 131 SIDE 2

A picture that shows this sentence

she got five fish.
she got five fish.
she got five fish.

hē has a fan.

shē is sick.

the man is in a car.

wē āte cōrn.

the cat has big fēēt.

Printed in the United States of America

66

NAME ______

TAKE-HOME 132 SIDE 1

1. the rabbit went down on his...

• fēēt   **• tāil**   • nōse

2. the rat slid down on his...

• fēēt   • tāil   **• nōse**

3. the rat got a sōre...

• nōse   • hand   • tāil

ī ī ī ī ī ī | d d d d d d
k k k k k k | r r r r r r
b b b b b b | g g g g g g

the girl went fōr a walk.
shē met a fat pig.

1. the girl went fōr a...

• walk   • pig   • talk

2. shē met a...

• fat pig   • little pig   • dog

TAKE-HOME 132 SIDE 2

A picture that shows this sentence

he slid on his nose.
he slid on his nose.
he slid on his nose.

this man is mad.

a rat ran.

the girl can run.

the dog has big ēars.

shē has a rāke.

Printed in the United States of America

NAME ____________________ TAKE-HOME 133 SIDE 1

1. the dog said, "pigs live…"

•on farms •on ships •in parks

2. the pig said, "I am a…"

•dog •rich pig •fat pig

3. the ship rocked and the dog…

•got wet •was fat •got sick

y y y y y y	k k k k k k
o o o o o o	i i i i i i
I I I I I I	b b b b b b

a girl went fishing.
shē did not get fish.

1. a girl went…

•hōme •running •fishing

2. shē did not get…

•sick •fish •fans

TAKE-HOME 133 SIDE 2

A picture that shows this sentence

I live on a ship.
I live on a ship.
I live on a ship.

hē sat on a log.

that dog has a hat.

shē fēēds the duck.

I am mad.

a little cat has fun.

Printed in the United States of America

NAME ____________________ TAKE-HOME 134 SIDE 1

1. the dog dug a hōle in the…

•lāke •cop •yard

2. did the man get mad?

•yes •nō

3. did the cop nēēd a cop dog?

•yes •nō

ō ō ō ō ō ō	k k k k k k
y y y y y y	ch ch ch ch
o o o o o o	w w w w w

a rat līkes to ēat.
hē ēats a red lēaf.

1. a rat līkes to…

•sit •ēat •run

2. hē ēats a…

•little lēaf •fat lēaf •red lēaf

TAKE-HOME 134 SIDE 2

A picture that shows this sentence

the dog dug a hole.
the dog dug a hole.
the dog dug a hole.

this fish is fat.

a dog sat on a rock.

wē are on a ship.

hē has a pot.

the gāte is big.

Printed in the United States of America

NAME ____________________

TAKE-HOME 135 SIDE 1

1. ron said,…

• "nō"   • "not"   **• "yes"**

2. did ron pāint the bed red?

• yes   • nō

3. did ron pāint a car red?

• yes   • nō

n n n n n n	y y y y y y
h h h h h h	u u u u u u
k k k k k k	m m m m m

a man went on a ship.
the ship was big.

1. a man went on a…

• hill   **• ship**   • cow

2. the ship was…

• big   • little   • red

TAKE-HOME 135 SIDE 2

A picture that shows this sentence

ron got the paint.
ron got the paint.
ron got the paint.

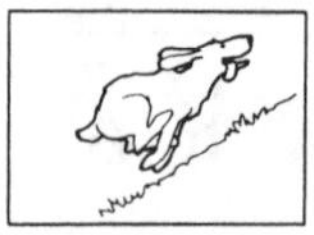

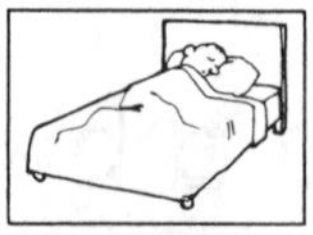

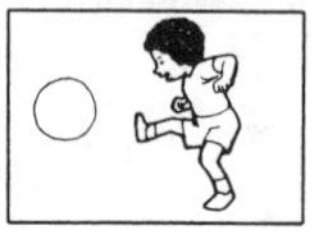

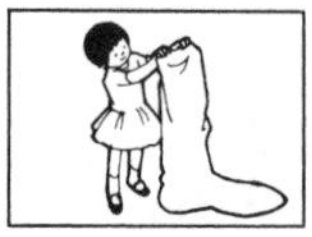

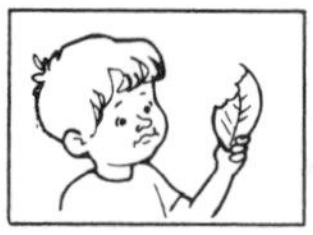

hē went to slēēp.

shē can kick.

a dog ran up a hill.

hē āte a lēaf.

this sock is big.

NAME ____________________

TAKE-HOME 136 SIDE 1

1. the bōy said, "let's gō to…"

• the ship   **• the park**   • the farm

2. the bōy said, "wē nēēd a…"

• cat   • park   **• car**

3. did they rīde to the park?

• yes   **• nō**

c c c c c c	f f f f f f
o o o o o o	s s s s s s
ē ē ē ē ē ē	g g g g g g

a dog dug a hōle.
a man fell in the hōle.

1. a dog dug a…

• hill   **• hōle**   • mōle

2. a man fell in the…

• lāke   • yard   **• hōle**

TAKE-HOME 136 SIDE 2

A picture that shows this sentence

they ran to the park.
they ran to the park.
they ran to the park.

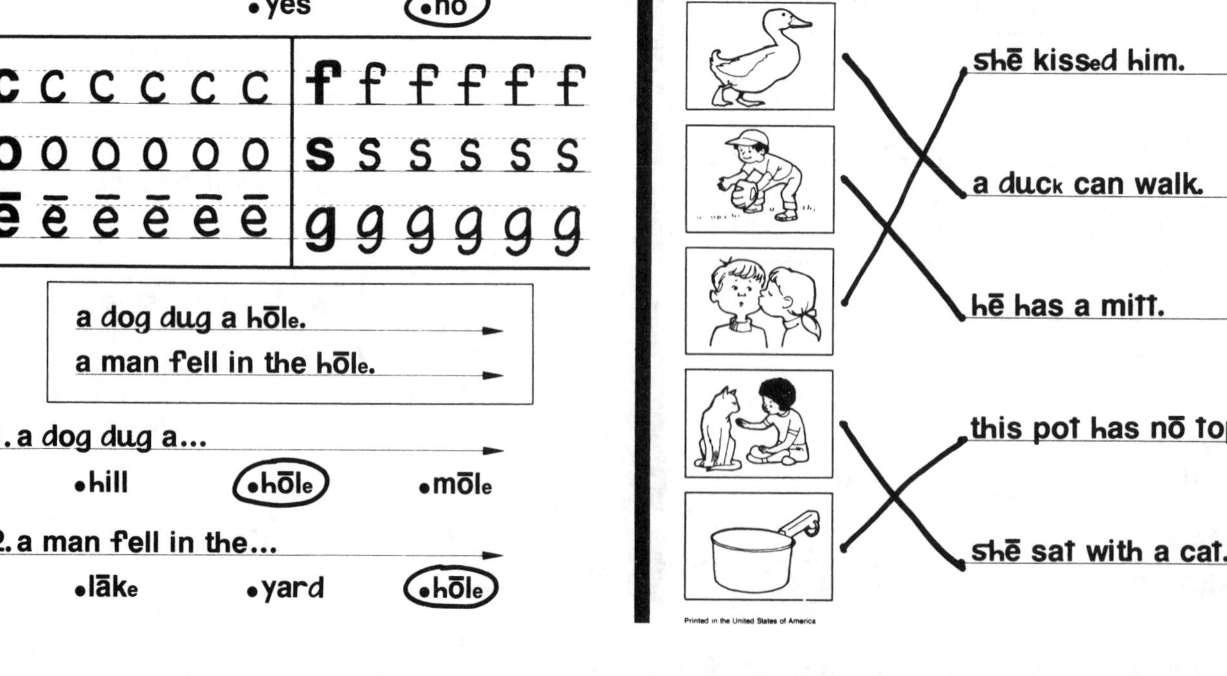

shē kissed him.

a duck can walk.

hē has a mitt.

this pot has nō top.

shē sat with a cat.

NAME ______________________ TAKE-HOME 137 SIDE 1

1. ann and her dad went hunting for...

- rabbits
- pigs
- deer

2. did the girl find a deer?

- yes
- no

3. the girl did not get a pet...

- dog
- deer
- cat

d d d d d d	o o o o o o
a a a a a a	g g g g g g
b b b b b b	p p p p p p

> a boy had red paint.
> so he made a car red.

1. a boy had red...

- pigs
- pots
- paint

2. so he made a car...

- red
- run
- road

TAKE-HOME 137 SIDE 2

A picture that shows this sentence

the girl has pets.
the girl has pets.
the girl has pets.

a cow will lick him.

he has no socks.

this hat is big.

she can dive.

that man is fishing.

Printed in the United States of America

NAME ______________________ TAKE-HOME 138 SIDE 1

1. a boy sent a card to his...

- mother
- brother
- dad

2. the cop gave the card to her...

- mother
- brother
- dad

3. a boy said, "give me that..."

- man
- card
- fish

p p p p p p	w w w w w
e e e e e e	ā ā ā ā ā ā
h h h h h h	ē ē ē ē ē ē

> a girl met a boy.
> she said, "let's dig a hole."

1. a girl met a...

- dog
- boy
- pig

2. she said, "let's..."

- sit
- run
- dig a hole

TAKE-HOME 138 SIDE 2

A picture that shows this sentence

he gave mom a card.
he gave mom a card.
he gave mom a card.

this bug is little.

she feeds the pig.

the goat ate a can.

that cop was mad.

he has a duck.

Printed in the United States of America

NAME ______________________ TAKE-HOME 139 SIDE 1

1. the ducks went fōr a...

•rīde •run (•walk)

2. they met a...

•mēan man (•mēan pig) •little bōy

3. did the pig ēat the ducks?

•yes (•nō)

f f f f f f | p p p p p p
k k k k k k | c c c c c c
t t t t t t | sh sh sh sh

a dēēr cāme up to them.
ann said, "are you a pet?"

1. a dēēr cāme up to...

(•them) •they •him

2. ann said, "are you..."

•a dog •a dēēr (•a pet)

TAKE-HOME 139 SIDE 2

A picture that shows this sentence

the ducks met a pig.
the ducks met a pig.
the ducks met a pig.

wē have hats.
that pig āte cōrn.
hē has a big rock.
the ōld man can run.
shē sat on a hill.

Printed in the United States of America

70

NAME ______________________ TAKE-HOME 140 SIDE 1

1. a bōy went to a...

•park (•tōy shop) •shōw

2. the bōy said, "I lIke..."

•big bōys •big dogs (•big tōys)

3. did the man have tōys fōr dogs?

(•yes) •nō

k k k k k k | e e e e e e
b b b b b b | u u u u u u
p p p p p p | l l l l l l

his mother got a card.
it said, "I love you."

1. his mother got a...

•car •farm (•card)

2. it said, "I..."

•hēar you (•love you) •sēē you

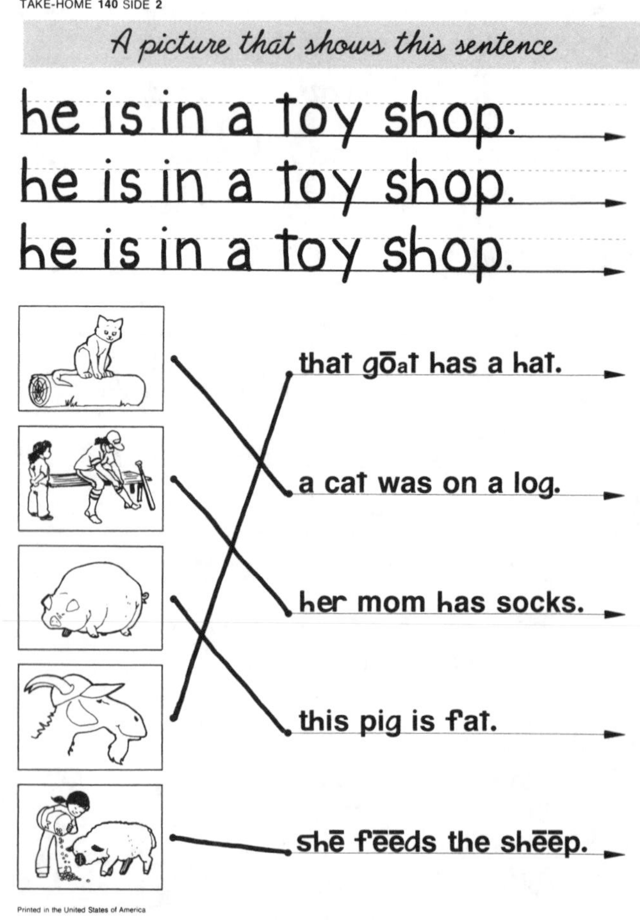

TAKE-HOME 140 SIDE 2

A picture that shows this sentence

he is in a toy shop.
he is in a toy shop.
he is in a toy shop.

that gōat has a hat.
a cat was on a log.
her mom has socks.
this pig is fat.
shē fēēds the shēēp.

Printed in the United States of America

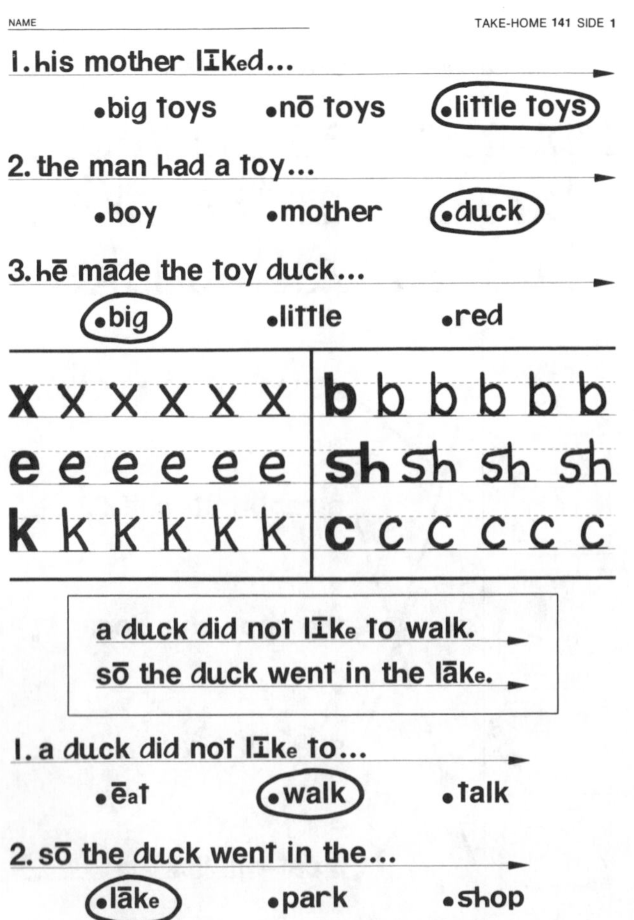

NAME ______________________ TAKE-HOME 141 SIDE 1

1. his mother līked...

- big toys
- nō toys
- (little toys)

2. the man had a toy...

- boy
- mother
- (duck)

3. hē māde the toy duck...

- (big)
- little
- red

x x x x x x | b b b b b b
e e e e e e | sh sh sh sh
k k k k k k | c c c c c c

a duck did not līke to walk.
sō the duck went in the lāke.

1. a duck did not līke to...

- ēat
- (walk)
- talk

2. sō the duck went in the...

- (lāke)
- park
- shop

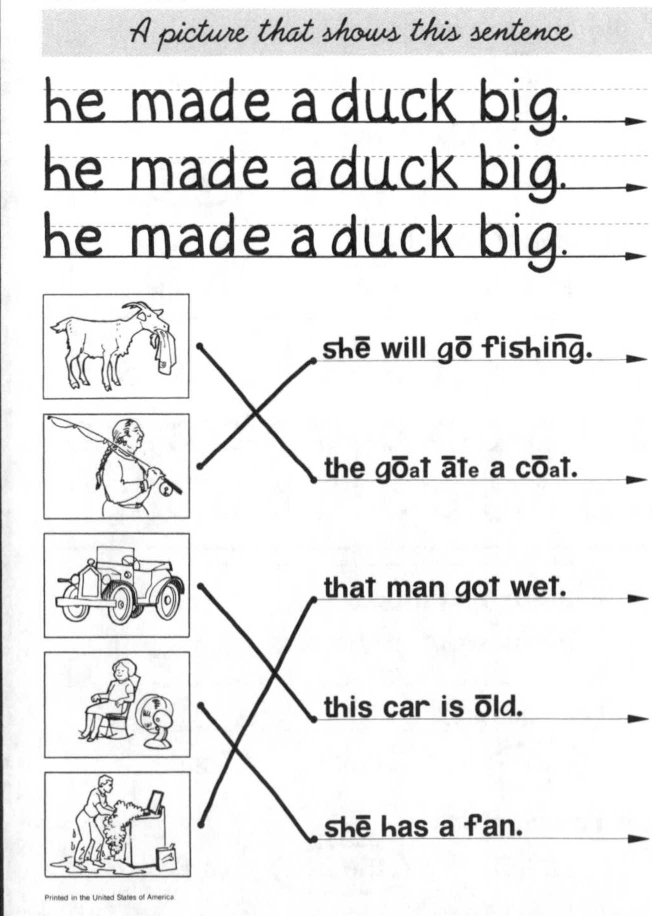

TAKE-HOME 141 SIDE 2

A picture that shows this sentence

he made a duck big.
he made a duck big.
he made a duck big.

shē will gō fishing.
the gōat āte a cōat.
that man got wet.
this car is ōld.
shē has a fan.

Printed in the United States of America

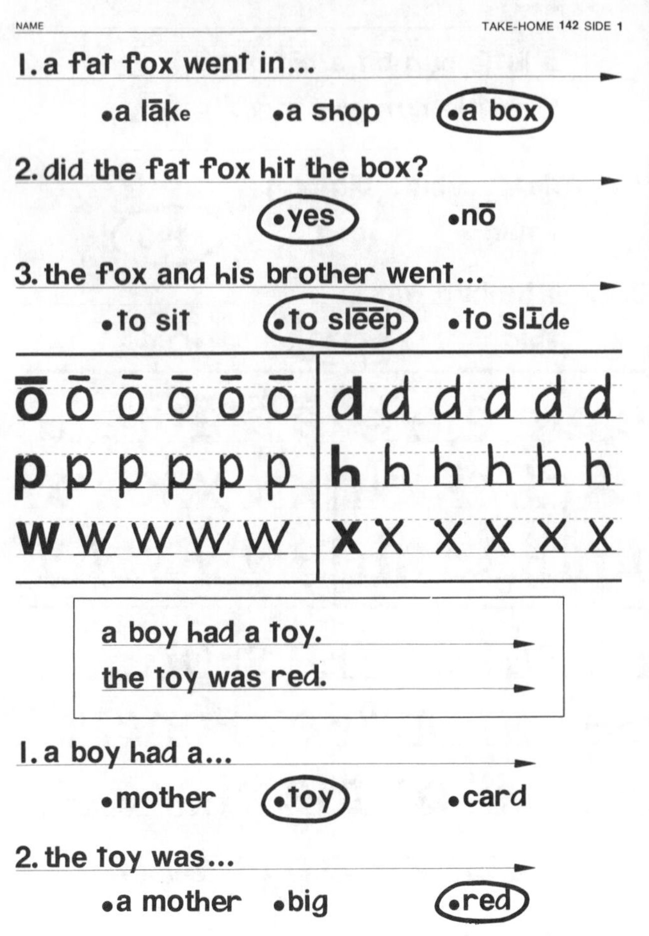

NAME ______________________ TAKE-HOME 142 SIDE 1

1. a fat fox went in...

- a lāke
- a shop
- (a box)

2. did the fat fox hit the box?

- (yes)
- nō

3. the fox and his brother went...

- to sit
- (to slēep)
- to slīde

ō ō ō ō ō ō | d d d d d d
p p p p p p | h h h h h h
w w w w w | x x x x x x

a boy had a toy.
the toy was red.

1. a boy had a...

- mother
- (toy)
- card

2. the toy was...

- a mother
- big
- (red)

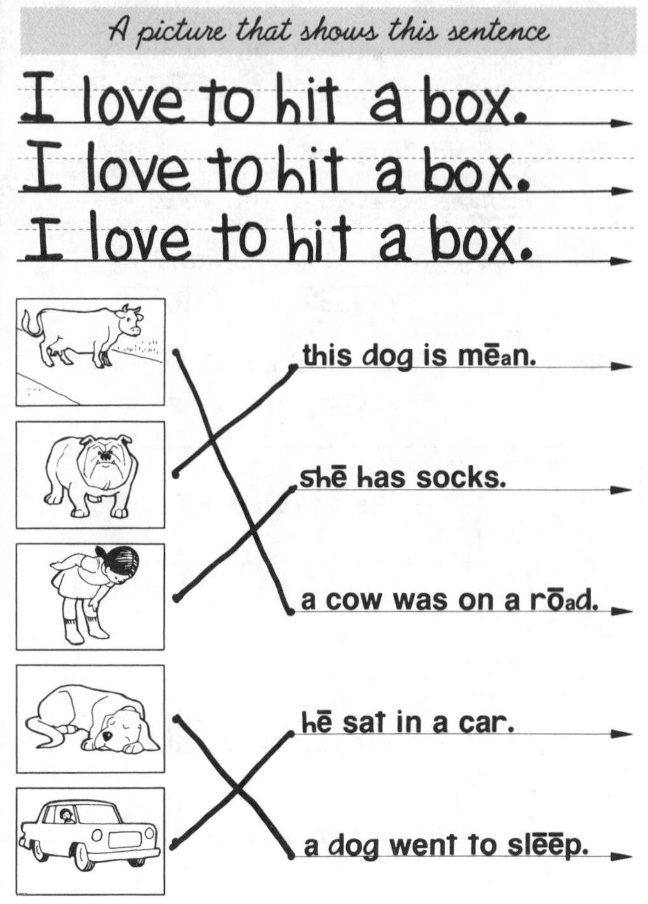

TAKE-HOME 142 SIDE 2

A picture that shows this sentence

I love to hit a box.
I love to hit a box.
I love to hit a box.

this dog is mēan.
shē has socks.
a cow was on a rōad.
hē sat in a car.
a dog went to slēep.

Printed in the United States of America

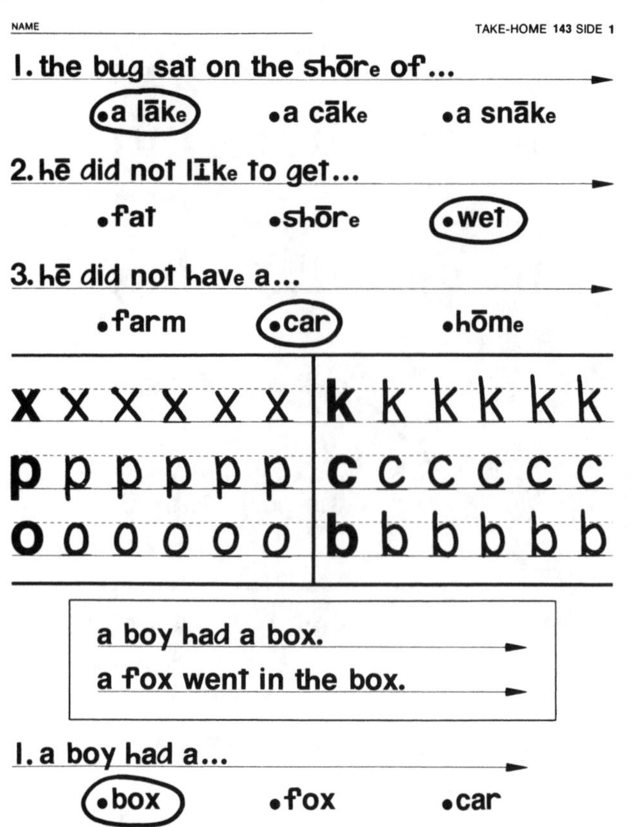

NAME ____________________

1. the bug sat on the shōre of...
   - a lāke (circled)
   - a cāke
   - a snāke
2. hē did not līke to get...
   - fat
   - shōre
   - wet (circled)
3. hē did not have a...
   - farm
   - car (circled)
   - hōme

x x x x x x	k k k k k k
p p p p p p	c c c c c c
o o o o o o	b b b b b b

a boy had a box.
a fox went in the box.

1. a boy had a...
   - box (circled)
   - fox
   - car
2. a fox went in...
   - a hōle
   - the box (circled)
   - a fox

A picture that shows this sentence

a bug sat at the lake.
a bug sat at the lake.
a bug sat at the lake.

a man sat on a rock.
a rabbit āte a lēaf.
the cop had a dog.
shē will dīve.
a cat will lick her.

Printed in the United States of America

NAME ____________________

1. a big ____ cāme and sat on the shōre.
   - rat
   - man
   - ēagle (circled)
2. the eagle said, "give mē a ____."
   - dīme (circled)
   - can
   - bug
3. did the bug give the eagle a dīme?
   - yes (circled)
   - nō
4. did the bug gō to the other sīde?

   - yes (circled)
   - nō

1. the man is fat.
2. hē has a fan.

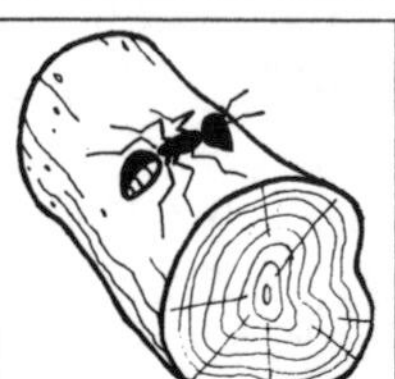

1. the bug is an ant.
2. the ant is on a log.

a little bug bit a big bug.
the little bug was mad.

1. a little ____ bit a big bug.
   - man
   - bag
   - bug (circled)
2. the little bug was ____.
   - big
   - mad (circled)
   - red

e e e e e e	ā ā ā ā ā ā
ch ch ch ch	x x x x x x
th th th th	y y y y y y

hē sat on the shōre.
he sat on the shore.
he sat on the shore.

A picture that shows this sentence

Printed in the United States of America

NAME ____________

1. a bug and a ____ met on a rōad.
   - (pig) • man • gōat
2. the bug bit a ____.
   - dog • (log) • bug
3. the pig bit ____.
   - (his leg) • the bug • a man
4. did the pig bīte better?
   - (yes) • nō

1. she has a cat.
2. they are on a rug.

1. the man is at the lāke.
2. hē has a fish.

hē līked to ēat.
sō hē āte bēans and cāke.

1. hē ____ to ēat.
   - hātes • (līked) • did not līke
2. sō hē āte bēans and ____.
   - cōrn • fish • (cāke)

t t t t t t | o o o o o o
i i i i i i | ī ī ī ī ī ī
e e e e e e | n n n n n n

"I bīte," a bug said.
"I bīte," a bug said.
"I bīte," a bug said.

A picture that shows this sentence

Printed in the United States of America

NAME ____________

1. a girl went to the shop with her ____.
   - car • (cat) • dog
2. then they went to the ____.
   - lāke • (park) • car
3. shē said, "you can not ____ to mē."
   - (talk) • walk • sit
4. did the cat talk?
   - (yes) • nō

1. the cat is sitting.
2. hē is on the bed.

1. the fish is not wet.
2. it is in the dish.

shē had a dog.
the dog did not talk.

1. shē had a ____.
   - log • bug • (dog)
2. the ____ did not talk.
   - fox • (dog) • bug

J J J J J J | d d d d d d
e e e e e e | y y y y y y
t t t t t t | x x x x x x

I can talk to you.
I can talk to you.
I can talk to you.

A picture that shows this sentence

Printed in the United States of America

NAME ________________ TAKE-HOME 147 SIDE 1

1. the girl said, "cats can not ____."
•talk •walk •slēēp

2. ann said, "can I have that ____?"
•can •cat •bug

3. the ____ said, "I will not gō with you."
•girl •ann •cat

4. ann said, "I will lēave this ____."
•park •dark •stōre

1. the man is a cop.

2. hē has a cat.

1. she has a dog.

2. they are on a log.

TAKE-HOME 147 SIDE 2

the man līked to swim.
sō hē jumped into the lāke.

1. the ____ līked to swim.
•boy •man •cow

2. sō hē ____ into the lāke.
•ran •jumped •fell

e e e e e e | n n n n n n
r r r r r r | t t t t t t
j j j j j j | f f f f f f

cats do not talk.
cats do not talk.
cats do not talk.

A picture that shows this sentence

Printed in the United States of America

NAME ________________ TAKE-HOME 148 SIDE 1

1. some girls went to the ____.
•shōre •moon •shop

2. a girl said, "I will fīnd some ____."
•fun •sun •nuts

3. the moon cow said, "come with ____."
•you •him •mē

4. the ____ jumped into the pool.
•man •boy •cow

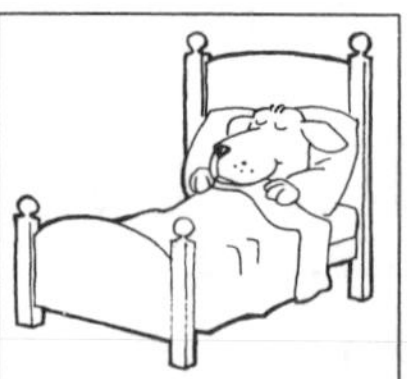

1. that dog is slēēping.

2. hē is in bed.

1. a toy is in her hand.

2. it is a toy ship.

TAKE-HOME 148 SIDE 2

the man had a pet cow.
hē talked to the cow.

1. the man had a pet ____.
•cat •car •cow

2. hē ____ to the cow.
•ran •talked •walked

d d d d d d | b b b b b b
p p p p p p | j j j j j j
y y y y y y | a a a a a a

shē went to the moon.
she went to the moon.
she went to the moon.

A picture that shows this sentence

Printed in the United States of America

NAME ____________________ TAKE-HOME 149 SIDE 1

1. the ōld car did not ____ .

- start (circled)
- stop
- shop

2. do rats have cars?

- yes
- nō (circled)

3. did the big man start the car?

- yes (circled)
- nō

4. the big man will kēēp sitting in ____ .

- the bus
- the cāve
- the car (circled)

1. a cat is on a pig.
2. they are on a bus.

1. a man is on the moon.
2. hē has a moon ship.

TAKE-HOME 149 SIDE 2

a girl went rīding in a car.
shē went to a farm.

1. a girl went ____ in a car.

- rīding (circled)
- talking
- walking

2. shē went to a ____ .

- farm (circled)
- park
- shop

e e e e e e | p p p p p p
m m m m m m | u u u u u u
g g g g g g | h h h h h h

the car did not start.
the car did not start.
the car did not start.

A picture that shows this sentence

Printed in the United States of America

NAME ____________________ TAKE-HOME 150 SIDE 1

1. an ōld ____ was in the barn.

- dog
- car
- hōrse (circled)

2. a ____ said, "have you sēēn a hōrse?"

- man (circled)
- car
- cat

3. did the ōld man fīnd a hōrse?

- yes (circled)
- nō

4. did the ōld hōrse līke to gō fōr a rīde?

- yes (circled)
- nō

1. the man is fat.
2. his car is ōld.

1. a cat is slēēping.
2. shē is on a log.

TAKE-HOME 150 SIDE 2

a girl had a hōrse.
shē went rīding on a hōrse.

1. a ____ had a hōrse.

- man
- gōat
- girl (circled)

2. shē went rīding on a ____ .

- hat
- hōrse (circled)
- gōat

u u u u u u | p p p p p p
J J J J J J | o o o o o o
y y y y y y | e e e e e e

they went riding.
they went riding.
they went riding.

A picture that shows this sentence

Printed in the United States of America

NAME ____________ TAKE-HOME 151 SIDE 1

1. bill līked to gō ____.

•rīding (•fishing) •hunting

2. bill did not get ____.

(•fish) •fat •mad

3. bill had a ____ on his līne.

•bug •rug (•tug)

4. bill had an ōld ____.

•boy •fish (•box)

1. this dog is mad.

2. a bug bit his leg.

1. shē is hot.

2. shē has a fan.

TAKE-HOME 151 SIDE 2

a girl went fishing.
shē got fīve fish.

1. a girl went ____.

•walking (•fishing) •running

2. shē got ____ fish.

(•fīve) •nīne •nō

ȳ ȳ ȳ ȳ ȳ ȳ | s s s s s s
p p p p p p | b b b b b b
r r r r r r | c c c c c c

bill did not get fish.
bill did not get fish.
bill did not get fish.

A picture that shows this sentence

Printed in the United States of America

NAME ____________ TAKE-HOME 152 SIDE 1

1. did bill get fish?

•yes (•nō)

2. the boys said, "you have an ōld ____."

•car (•box) •fox

3. bill said, "that box is filled with ____."

•fish •boys (•gōld)

4. bill was ____.

(•not sad) •a bug •gōld

1. the cop is on a hōrse.

2. the hōrse has a hat.

1. shē got a fish.

2. hē got a can.

TAKE-HOME 152 SIDE 2

a man went in a sāil bōat.
hē had a lot of fun.

1. a man went in a ____.

(•sāil bōat) •little bōat •sāil gōat

2. hē had a lot ____.

•of bōats (•of fun) •of cows

ī ī ī ī ī ī | a a a a a a
o o o o o o | u u u u u u
i i i i i i | e e e e e e

"it is gōld," hē said.
"it is gold," he said.
"it is gold," he said.

A picture that shows this sentence

Printed in the United States of America

NAME ______________________ TAKE-HOME 153 SIDE 1

1. the ēagle said, "I līke to ____."

run **•flȳ** •fish

2. the hōrse said, "can you ____ mē to flȳ?"

•love •wish **•tēach**

3. did the hōrse flȳ to the top of a barn?

•yes **•nō**

4. hē ran into the ____ of the barn.

•sīde •top •back

1. the man has a bug.

2. the bug is on his hat.

1. that cat is slēeping.

2. shē is on a rug.

TAKE-HOME 153 SIDE 2

an ēagle līked to flȳ.

hē did not sit in a trēē.

1. an ēagle līked ____.

•to ēat •to sit **•to flȳ**

2. hē did not sit in ____.

•a trēē •a park •a bed

b b b b b b | v v v v v v

k k k k k k | f f f f f f

j j j j j j | i i i i i i

an eagle līkes to flȳ.

an eagle likes to fly.

an eagle likes to fly.

A picture that shows this sentence

Printed in the United States of America

NAME ______________________ TAKE-HOME 154 SIDE 1

1. did the hōrse flȳ to the top of a car?

•yes **•nō**

2. the hōrse ran into the ____ of the car.

•top **•sīde** •back

3. the hōrse ran with the ēagle on his ____.

•top •sīde **•back**

4. did they have fun?

•yes •nō

1. this dog is in a car.

2. a cat is on the car.

1. this pig has fun.

2. hē is in the mud.

TAKE-HOME 154 SIDE 2

an ōld car did not run.

the girl got mad at the car.

1. an ōld ____ did not run.

•cat **•car** •cow

2. the girl got ____ at the car.

•bad •sad **•mad**

p p p p p p | h h h h h h

x x x x x x | k k k k k k

ȳ y y ȳ ȳ ȳ | j j j j j j

the hōrse ran.

the horse ran.

the horse ran.

A picture that shows this sentence

Printed in the United States of America

NAME ______________________ TAKE-HOME 155 SIDE 1

1. shē brushed her tēēth ____ tīmes a dāy.
•nīne •six •nō

2. shē had a ____ tooth brush.
•toy •red •gōld

3. did her tēēth shīne līke the moon?
•yes •nō

4. did her mother have the tooth brush?
•yes •nō

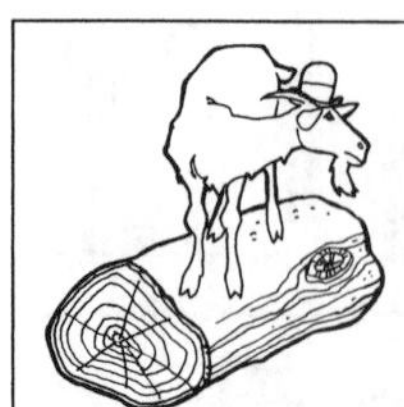

1. the gōat is on a log.

2. hē has a hat.

1. this man is a cop.

2. hē is fat.

TAKE-HOME 155 SIDE 2

bill had a brush.
it was not a tooth brush.

1. bill had a ______.
•brush •car •bat

2. was it a tooth brush?
•yes •nō

qu qu qu
c c c c c c
b b b b b b
d d d d d d
f f f f f f
g g g g g g

I nēēd a tooth brush.
I need a tooth brush.
I need a tooth brush.

A picture that shows this sentence

NAME ______________________ TAKE-HOME 156 SIDE 1

1. the girl slipped on her ____.
•rug •fēēt •dog

2. the dog was brushing his ____.
•tēēth •nōse •fēēt

3. the dog had the red ____ brush.
•hand •tooth •nāil

4. did the dog's tēēth shīne now?
•yes •nō

1. that bug is an ant.

2. it is on a can.

1. shē has a dog.

2. they are on the rug.

TAKE-HOME 156 SIDE 2

bill went to the park.
hē went in the big pool.

1. bill went to the ____.
•pond •farm •park

2. hē went in the ____ pool.
•bad •big •little

qu qu qu
x x x x x x
k k k k k k
ō ō ō ō ō ō
ā ā ā ā ā ā
ȳ ȳ ȳ ȳ ȳ ȳ

the girl smīled.
the girl smiled.
the girl smiled.

A picture that shows this sentence

NAME ______________________

TAKE-HOME 157 SIDE 1

1. an ēagle āte cāke and ham and ____.
- nuts
- (cōrn)
- bēans

2. hē got ____.
- (fatter)
- better
- sadder

3. a little eagle sat ____ a trēē.
- on
- (under)
- at

4. then a ____ cāme hunting fōr ēagles.
- man
- boy
- (tīger)

1. this cat is slēēping.
2. shē is in bed.

1. the man is sitting.
2. hē is on a fish.

TAKE-HOME 157 SIDE 2

a girl līked to talk.
shē talked to the māil man.

1. a girl līked ____.
- to walk
- to sit
- (to talk)

2. shē talked to the ____.
- (māil man)
- sad man
- moon man

J J J J J J	y y y y y y
z z z z z z	e e e e e e
k k k k k k	r r r r r r

a fat eagle sat.
a fat eagle sat.
a fat eagle sat.

A picture that shows this sentence

Printed in the United States of America

79

NAME ______________________

TAKE-HOME 158 SIDE 1

1. the fat ēagle cāme down on the ____.
- ēagle
- (tīger)
- hōrse

2. the ____ ran far awāy.
- ēagle
- (tīger)
- boy

3. do the ēagles māke fun of the fat ēagle?
- yes
- (nō)

4. they give him ____ and ham and cōrn.
- cans
- nuts
- (cāke)

1. this dog runs.
2. shē has a hat.

1. the man is a cop.
2. his car is ōld.

TAKE-HOME 158 SIDE 2

a tīger sat under a trēē.
hē was looking fōr rabbits.

1. a tīger sat ____ a trēē.
- in
- nēar
- (under)

2. hē was looking fōr ____.
- girls
- (rabbits)
- pigs

z z z z z z	n n n n n n
f f f f f f	e e e e e e
u u u u u u	r r r r r r

they gave him cake.
they gave him cake.
they gave him cake.

A picture that shows this sentence

Printed in the United States of America

NAME ______________________ TAKE-HOME 159 SIDE 1

1. a man līked to ____.

•slēēp •fish (•gō fast)

2. did hē talk fast?

(•yes) •nō

3. the egg slipped and fell on his ____.

•head (•fēēt) •nōse

4. the mēat pīe hit his ____.

•mother  •fēēt

1. that pig is wet.

2. hē is in the mud.

1. this man is hot.

2. hē has a fan.

TAKE-HOME 159 SIDE 2

a girl walked down the rōad.
shē met a big fox.

1. a girl ____ down the rōad.

•looked (•walked) •ran

2. shē met a big ____.

•log (•fox) •dog

z z z z z z	m m m m m
ū ū ū ū ū ū	n n n n n n
b b b b b b	r r r r r r

hē āte a mēat pīe.
he ate a meat pie.
he ate a meat pie.

A picture that shows this sentence

80

NAME ______________________ TAKE-HOME 160 SIDE 1

1. the ____ said, "Ī will slōw down."

•mother •wīfe (•man)

2. sō hē did not gō ____ in his car.

•rīding (•fast) •slōw

3. did hē walk fast?

•yes 

4. did hē ēat fast?

•yes 

1. the man is at the lāke.

2. hē is on a log.

1. that dog is sitting.

2. shē is on a bed.

TAKE-HOME 160 SIDE 2

hē fell in the mud.
his nōse had mud on it.

1. hē ____ in the mud.

•walked •sat (•fell)

2. his ____ had mud on it.

(•nōse) •hat •fēēt

o o o o o o	k k k k k k
ū ū ū ū ū ū	t t t t t t
f f f f f f	g g g g g g

"Ī ēat fast," hē said.
"I eat fast," he said.
"I eat fast," he said.

A picture that shows this sentence